When Emotions Lie

Deondriea Cantrice

Way, Inc
Prosper, Texas

This book is a work of fiction. The events and characters described herein are imaginary and are not intended to refer to specific places or living persons. The opinions expressed in this manuscript are solely the opinions of the author and do not represent the opinions or thoughts of the publisher.

Dedication

To my children Tyler, C'erra and Dietrich, in life you can choose to do whatever you want to. But you never get to choose the consequences.

5

Acknowledgments

*To David and Frankie Charles,
thank you for all of your love and support.*

A very special thanks to Madeline Bynes, Jori Moore and Carrie Schara. I value your friendship, appreciate you for challenging me to expand my talents and allowing me to be me.

Blind Sided

My heart sank, time was suspended, and I felt a sharp pain pierce through my soul. I stood there breathless and speechless, while my children ran up to this young woman yelling,

"Miss Piper we miss you, come see our dad and say hi to our mom."

All at once I had a million thoughts flash through my head, everything from turning around and walking away, to snatching my husband by his throat and using him to knock the hell out of this woman. But I was frozen. I could not muster a single word or gesture. Everything was a blur. The hustle and bustle of the store became a dull murmur. I saw my children jump into this woman's arms and ask could they spend the night again. What was I supposed to think, what was I supposed to say?

There we were standing in the middle of the grocery store so if I snatched this raggedy heffa up by her hair, I would probably wind up in jail and my husband would most likely take my children back to *Miss Piper's house* while I was locked up. But I had to do something. I needed to know who this over-weight, poorly dressed, no make-up havin' on, woman was.

Being the lady, my granny taught me to be, I quickly gathered my composure, extended my hand to this woman and with a pasted on smile I said, "I am Mrs. Alicia Rowe,

Arlington's wife and you are?" The woman looked at my hand, shook it timidly and said,

"I am Piper Middleton. It's a pleasure to meet you."

"Well Piper, what is your acquaintance with my husband and children?" There was an unpleasant moment of fumbling silence while Piper and my husband looked back and forth at one another. Ok was I speaking Greek or something because I know I didn't stutter or whisper. I know she heard what I said. With the biggest smile on my face, I politely asked again,

"What is the nature of your relationship with my husband?"

The scared look on Piper's face immediately turned smug as she answered,

"I'm his woman. We've been seeing each other for about a year."

I knew things were about to get ugly, so I began to pray silently. *Lord, please don't let me kill her, I only intend to hurt her really bad, forgive me Lord; she knows not what I am about to do.* Looking at her in utter amazement and disgust I asked,

"How in the hell can you be with someone who is married, or did you not know he was married?" Nonchalantly Piper replied,

"Yeah, I know Arlington is married, but it's not my fault that his wife doesn't know how to keep her husband happy and at home."

The hair on the back of my neck stood up, my nostrils flared, and my lips tightened. I could not believe this oversized, poorly dressed, nappy-headed heffa was trying to get buck with me. All I could do to refrain from slapping the hell out of her was to grab my husband by the hand and say,

"Bring your ass, now damn it."

The children scurried behind Arlington and I, as we hastily walked out of the store leaving the entire cart of groceries behind. I trembled inside as we loaded into our SUV. I have never been more angry and embarrassed in my life. We rode out of the parking lot in silence; I was so disgusted with Arlington that I couldn't form as much as a syllable. The silence only perpetuated the tension between me and him.

Luckily for Arlington, I refused to act a fool in front of my children. I couldn't begin to explain to them what was going on. With one hand on the wheel, I began digging inside my purse with my other hand to find my cell phone, with just one hand; I managed to dial my parent's house.

"Hey mom it's Alicia, are you busy? Is it ok if I bring the children over for the evening?"

"Sure we don't have anything going on."

"Alright, thanks for letting me bring them over we should be there in 15 minutes or so."

"See you, then."

After the conversation with my mother ended, I threw my phone back in my purse. My mother was always delighted to have my children over. Sometimes I think the only reason she had children was so that one day she could become a grandmother. One day she told me, God ordained her into the position of grandma. My children were her only grandkids and they got away with things that I still better not think about even as an adult.

Smooth Jazz softly played in the background and silence filled the truck. The children didn't mutter a sound even after they heard that they were going to grandma's house. Driving down the highway, all I did was second-guess myself in my mind. Did I do the right thing by walking away? Should I have beaten that woman down? Should I have cussed my husband out?

They say a woman should always behave like a lady in public but, whoever thought that up never encountered a situation like this one. I think this situation warranted me to act an ass and entitled me to a get out of jail free card. I desperately wanted to turn my SUV around, find that woman and ring her damn neck.

Arriving at my mother's house in record time, I let the children out at the end of the driveway and waved them off as my mother stood in the door. There was no way my mother could see me like this. She would have immediately known that something was wrong. I can't lie to my mother. If I told her what just happened, she would have had my dad get the nine and ask no questions.

I really didn't know what I was more upset about, was it that he exposed my kids to her, the fact that he was cheating, how I found out, or that he cheated on me with one of the tackiest women I have seen in ages?

After leaving my parent's house, I drove around the corner and pulled over at a park, turned the truck and asked,

"What in the hell just happened? I need to understand why? Not only have you been cheating on me for a year, you stand there like a sorry bastard as she disrespected me; you took my children around her. Explain that to me!"

Arlington looked at me as if he had been rehearsing his story in his head. As if he anticipated the arrival of this day and responded.

"I admit taking the kids over her house was probably a mistake, but believe me I never had sex with that woman, we are just friends."

Call me Sally Sausage Head, I thought to myself. He must really think I am that stupid.

"No Arlington sleeping with her once is a mistake, sleeping with her for a year is a freaking habit. That still doesn't explain why in the hell would you ever expose my children to her?"

With a stupid look on his face Arlington answered,

"Alicia you were in Japan on business, Eric and the fellas called me so we could hang out, and Ariah needed her hair done. I killed two birds with one stone. She did Ariah's hair for me and babysat while I hung out. It was late when I got back so rather than waking them up and risking a DUI, we stayed all night. That was the only time I took them over there. None of that matters now. Look, I made a mistake. I admit I was wrong and I'm sorry."

"What exactly are you sorry about Arlington? Are you sorry for cheating? Or, are you sorry that I found out you have been lying to me for the past year? And, I don't buy that sad excuse of a story since we both have friends and family across this damn state. Better yet there are more hair salons than there are gas stations around here."

"I'm sorry for everything. I would never do anything to hurt you but none of that is important right now, I love you, and all that is in the past."

"No Arlington that is not in the past. That was up close, personal, and talking to me in the damn store. Why do you think lying to me and cheating on me wouldn't hurt me? How can you lie to me with a straight face?"

I was so disgusted with Arlington I didn't even care to hear his reply. I started my SUV and drove off. I began to ponder my next move. No book I have ever read, class I've attended, or life experience prepared me for this moment. I could not describe what I was feeling or how to handle my emotions. Arlington sat quiet but I noticed him trying to discreetly silence his cell phone vibrating in his pocket.

"Go ahead and answer her call. It's not like you ain't gon' call her the first moment I'm not around. I'll take you home so you can handle your business. You know what, go ahead call Piper and tell her you got to lay low for a while, but you will be in touch soon, or whatever the hell you raggedy ass men tell your hoes when you get caught."

Arlington shook his head. He was obviously upset and frustrated. But why in the hell was he so irritated? He's been playing house with my kids and another woman.

"Alicia will you shut up long enough to listen to me? I will explain everything to you."

"Listen to you for what Arlington? Listen to you lie to me? Listen to you tell me she is some worthless hoe that you don't give a damn about? I know the game, when a man gets busted the first thing out of his mouth is *she didn't mean anything to me, she's just some hoe I was messing with.*"

"You know what Alicia, never mind. I'm not gonna argue with you. Whenever you get through tripping, holla at me."

Arlington turned up the radio and starred out the window. Here comes the player move. Arlington is trying to rethink his strategy. I can see it coming. He is either going to play the *yeah I cheated because you are not taking care of me like a wife is supposed to card* or the *Billy bad ass, either accept it or don't card.* Either way it goes, he will not get off that easy.

We rode in silence for the next twenty minutes. Arriving at the house I stopped the truck and said,

"I'll be back; I have to go get my head together." Arlington looked at me and said,

"That's probably a good thing. You really need to bring it down a couple notches. We'll talk about this after you get your mouth under control. I will not go back and forth with a bunch of emotionally charged insults with you. I love you so we need to handle our business. And, for the record, I have no idea who is calling my phone but whoever it is can wait. You and the kids are what matters to me now."

With a blank look I replied,

"If this is how you treat the people you love, I'm so damn glad that you don't hate me. Arlington I can't talk to you right now so it's best that I go. You sure have a lot to say now that your girlfriend ain't around. When you were standing in front of her your 235-pound spineless ass didn't have a damn thing to say. What's up? Were you trying to protect her feelings? Or were you trying to keep her from busting you out? Please get the hell out my truck."

With hesitation Arlington took a deep sigh and got out. Before shutting the door he replied,

"You know damn well; I don't do drama. I was protecting you and the kids by not letting a situation develop. I will not let you try to emasculate me because you disagree with my decision."

I rolled my eyes and put my truck in gear. Arlington slammed the truck door. Through my rearview mirror I saw him answer his cell phone as I drove off.

I needed to go where I could gather myself. Senor Juan's was the answer. This was my favorite happy hour spot. It was a quaint little Mexican restaurant where the top shelf margaritas were two for one, the appetizers were great, and there was never the possibility of running into anyone I knew. The crowd wasn't the best, but it was mellow, and they served liquor, chips and salsa. This was the best place for me to unwind and collect my thoughts.

After I inhaled my first margarita, I called my friends Cassie and Myra to meet me. Cassie was my girl straight from the hood. Her parents moved to the right side of the tracks when she was a junior in high school. It was too late; the streets were already embedded in her. No matter how much money Cassie made, where she lived, what she was doing, or what she was wearing, Cassie was always ready to get buck at the drop of a hat.

Cassie and I met in college. She was there on a partial cheerleading scholarship. She only went to college so she could move out of her momma's house and party with a reason. She never planned to go to college. Cassie assumed because she looked good, she would marry rich so there was no need to learn anything other than how to be cute.

Cassie and I pledged Zeta Delta Sigma together and she has been my girl ever since. Cassie got her degree, but worked as a manager at a fast-food joint until her aunt Carol got her a job at a law firm. Until she got that job at the firm, Cassie was convinced working in corporate America made her a sellout. Somehow her aunt and I explained that white people owned fast food restaurants too. The only difference between the fast-food industry and corporate America is in corporate America you are respected more and get paid better.

Cassie had so much going for herself. She stood about 5'7, had a nice caramel complexion, built like a brick house, and owned the best of everything money could buy. The funny thing about Cassie was her intelligence was her best asset. I mean she had the intellect of a professor. But to her, being cute and popular were more important than being intelligent until she discovered intellect was attractive to the elite men in Denver.

My dear friend Myra on the other hand has read every self-help book on the market and even worse she was "saved" so you know what that meant. If she wasn't quoting scriptures or singing a hymn, she was reciting wisdom from some PhD that had never been through anything but college but has the nerve to give advice based upon case studies. There is nothing wrong with being saved, after all I am. But this woman pleads the blood of Jesus over everything. I know He shed his blood for us, but how many pints of blood did she think the man had?

Myra and I have been friends so long; I don't even remember how we met or why we were friends because we didn't have very much in common. Myra was in her late 20's and still a virgin because she was waiting for the Lord to send her a husband, like the Lord was gonna drop her a man from the sky. Meanwhile, she sat on every board and committee imaginable.

I personally believed Myra was only involved in all the extracurricular activities to mask her loneliness. I don't care what a woman says; a fulfilling career or active "volunteer networking life" does not replace a man. I have never heard of a woman having an orgasm because she is a volunteer chairperson or because she works 60 plus hours a week. And, check stubs for damn sure can't hold you at night.

Myra was natural, a diamond in the rough if you will. She had a complexion as dark and smooth as chocolate, with long, thick, pretty hair that she always had snatched back in a bun. Myra was beautiful but she never wore makeup or let her hair down unless there was some great and moving event like Jakes being in town, or an annual convention. In fact, I think my wedding 5 years ago was the last time I saw her hair done and wearing makeup.

I thought it was a bright idea to call both Cassie and Myra because I knew that somewhere in the midst of their neuroticism, I would be able to figure out my next step and find a solution to my dilemma. Besides, I am a little sadistic; bringing them together would be entertaining to me and would definitely prompt laughter. I loved to listen to them argue, they could push each other's buttons.

It was downright funny to watch them passionately bicker about things neither one of them really cared about but they both wanted to be heard and be right. Even if I didn't discover an answer to my dilemma, I would at least be entertained for a couple of hours.

Both Myra and Cassie were willing to meet me. As I waited for them to arrive, I knew I needed to cry but I could not find the tears. My mind was so scattered that I could not focus on a single thought or know exactly what my heart was feeling. I was just numb inside. I couldn't wrap my mind around the past few hours of events. I woke up this morning walking on sunshine, now I felt like I was in the pit of hell.

I am not mad at Piper for wanting Arlington; he was definitely the cat's meow. He had an unyielding swagger, the body of a Greek god, intelligent, made big money, a good father, and he can put it down, all the way down. And, let's not forget he married me, so that proves he has great judgment. That is why I can't understand why he would do something this stupid. Let the truth be told, I am the prize to be won. There ain't another woman out there better than me so, all he could do is settle for someone less and get caught up in some BS.

Cassie and Myra arrived at Senor Juan's at the same time only to find me with my forehead planted in my hands. Before I could say anything, Myra took one look at me and asked,

"What happened? Don't tell me you lost your job?"

I took a deep breath, "I wish it was that simple. Order your drinks first. You will need a couple drinks to stomach this story."

Cassie signaled the waitress to come to our table. She ordered a full round for us and water with lemon for Myra. The ladies got comfortable and turned off their mobile phones and situated the table. The waitress returned with our drinks. I raised my glass to toast,

"Drink up ladies, I just found out that Arlington has been cheating for the past year. We bumped into his hoe while we were shopping with the kids."

Neither one of the ladies raised their glass to toast. They put their glasses down without taking a sip. Puzzled, Myra looked at Cassie then back at me,

"What did you just say?"

"You heard correctly, Arlington has been cheating on me."

I began to tell the story of what happened, before I could complete the story, Cassie blurts,

"OH HELL NAW! Let's roll, whose whip we about to rock? That bitch is about to catch a beat down!"

"Why she gotta be a bitch? Beat her down for what? Alicia is married to Arlington not to this Piper chick. What is beating up the other woman going to do other than make both of these women look like some stupid fools? This ain't Jerry Springer. That's not how grown, intelligent, Christian people handle business." Myra interjected.

"If it don't teach her nothing else, it will teach her not to mess with nobody else's husband. It will damn sure teach her what an ass whoopin feels like. And, she's a bitch, a hoe, a slut, and trifling for screwing with somebody else's husband."

Myra raised her eyebrow, shook her head and replied,

"And what about Arlington? It takes two to tangle. Are we going to beat up every woman he messes with? Not to excuse Piper but, Arlington is the one in the wrong. He is the one that pledged to love, honor and respect till death do them part. Besides I'm grown, I quit fighting in high school. I believe that everything happens for a reason and the Word declares vengeance is mine said the Lord."

"Do you believe God uses people? That we are vessels?"

"Yes, of course."

"Then believe that God is using me to execute His vengeance on her ass."

Listening to Myra and Cassie go back and forth only gave me a headache this time. Their banter was not amusing or encouraging in the least. I still had no idea what I was feeling or what in the hell I was about to do.

"Ladies I have to go home and think about this. Let's table this discussion and have another round." I insisted.

They both looked at me as if I was crazy, but what could I say? We sat for the next few minutes engaging in surface conversation until Cassie once again blurted,

"Why are we sitting here acting like nothing happened? Arlington needs to be cussed the hell out and his hoe needs to be beat down."

I just rubbed my forehead as I shook my head back and forth.

"Right now I don't know what I am going to do. I never thought my life would be a talk show headline."

After three margaritas and a shot of tequila, I was ready to go home and face Arlington.

"I'm telling you what you should do. You should beat that hoe down and make Arlington pay out his ass. He'd go broke buying me I'm sorry gifts." Cassie said.

"Thanks for the suggestion, Cassie, but I have to go home now and deal with this situation, thank you for your support and I promise I will call ya'll later."

I dropped some money on the table and headed for the exit before Cassie or Myra could respond.

I can only imagine the conversation that went on at the table once I walked out. I knew they were there talking about me but it was time for me to face this situation head on.

Driving home I tried to prepare myself to see Arlington. I was ready to handle whatever he was going to dish out, so I thought. I honestly thought he would be in the streets somewhere trying to make up with Piper. Instead, I walked in to find him sitting in the family room.

"Alicia I am so glad you came home. Sit down so we can talk. Baby, you go to know that I love you. I was wrong and I am sorry I should have never befriended her, but believe me when I tell you that I never slept with her. Let me tell you the story from the beginning" Arlington said remorsefully.

"I am glad you are sorry. Only a sorry bastard would jeopardize a happy home for a piece of street bootie. If she was lying why didn't you call her out then, rather than confessing now? Please Arlington, I have heard enough from your lying ass."

I tuned Arlington out as if he wasn't even in there. I placed my keys on the table, flipped through the mail, then headed upstairs, entered the master bedroom, took off my clothes, put on pajamas, tied my hair up, removed my makeup and got in the bed without acknowledging Arlington's presence.

All the while Arlington followed me around trying to apologize insisting that we call her so she could tell the truth. Everything he said to me was just noise to me, shallow empty words. There was nothing he could say that would ease the humiliation and rage that I was feeling.

"I better go get an AIDS test because no telling what that nasty heffa got. I know you were running raw and you are a selfish bastard that would bring something home that you didn't leave here with."

"Alicia I know you are hurt but you are talking crazy. I told you, I have never came close to having sex with her. Yes, she and I hung out and she helped me with the kids when you were gone but I promise you that's it!"

"I see having a hoe on the side is teaching you how to lie better. Good Night Arlington, I don't want you near me go sleep in the guest room, on the couch, Piper's house or wherever as long as it's not next to me."

I rolled over, turning my back to him. Arlington walked out the bedroom, slamming the door behind him.

I tossed and turned all night. My nerves just wouldn't let me sleep. Was I embarrassed, angry, stupid or what? I didn't see the signs that my husband actually had a side thang going. Then to add insult to injury she was not cute.

It was barely the crack of dawn. I decided to get up since I couldn't sleep anyway. I got dressed quietly, I was not about to start my day off with Arlington's tall tales. All night I heard him say that he loved me, but his actions screamed a different story. I believe he was trying to convince himself that he didn't love this other woman.

Before I crept out of the house, I saw Arlington fast asleep on the loveseat of the family room where he had spent the night. I watched him sleep peacefully for a while. I contemplated whether I should slap his face or throw a bucket of hot grits on him. He did not deserve to sleep in peace after all I didn't. We wouldn't be in this situation if it wasn't for him. Damn his sorry ass! I know I was thinking crazy so I left the house before I did something stupid like punch him in the throat.

Arlington and I got married five years ago and had two beautiful children. Ariah that was five and Arlington's namesake that we called AJ was six. I made Arlington into what he is. When we met he was moving from job to job with no benefits, 401k, a degree or any real skill sets. After we got married, I called in a favor from a dealer/principal that I knew that gave Arlington a job. I made Arlington get a degree; with it he began to climb the corporate ladder.

After moving up the ranks of our organizations, we both branched out and formed our own companies. Both of our companies have been exceptionally lucrative. We lived deep in the suburbs of Denver where we owned a 6,500 square foot home. We drove matching Range Rovers and owed a 500 series Benz. I must add our bank account and credit scores ignited envy. I had done pretty well for myself and I'll be damned if I give it all up to a raggedy heffa that didn't care enough about herself to even have her nails done. Last night I was numb, but this morning, I can feel the rage flowing through my veins.

Playing Not to Lose

Leaving my house when the sun barely lit the sky, I headed to Ms. Shirley's house. Ms. Shirley used to be the children's nanny and was like a surrogate mother to me. I knew that she would understand what I was going through and could give me some sound advice as to what my next move should be. Her house was a good choice because I knew she was the only other person that would be up at 6am on a Saturday morning. I swear Ms. Shirley woke up each day and pushed the sun up.

Knocking as I walked through the back door into the kitchen, I saw Ms. Shirley. Just as I thought, she was dressed in her flowered print, pastel colored duster, sitting at the kitchen table dipping the crusts of her toast in her coffee as she read her daily devotional. Looking up from her book Ms. Shirley said,

"Hey baby come on in, I'm just finishing up breakfast. Can I get you something to eat?"

Ms. Shirley was just country. She had a standard routine, she woke up each morning, unlocked the door and cooked breakfast. Just like the sun rose each morning you could bet Ms. Shirley was eating eggs, a strip of bacon, or sausage link, a slice of toast, orange juice, and coffee. If she wanted variety she might make a teaspoon of grits. I would think she would be bored eating the same thing day after day, year after year. But she was always content. I hated that she unlocked the door each morning especially in this day and age. But I lost that argument years ago, so it doesn't even bother me anymore.

"What's on your mind?" Ms. Shirley asked as she looked over her reading glasses at me.

"I'm ok; I just stopped by to check on you."

"You didn't have to come and check on me at 6 o'clock in the morning you could have called."

Ms. Shirley continued to stare over the top of her glasses. I knew what that meant. We would sit staring at each other until I said something. I guess I better get it over with and tell her why I'm here.

"I don't understand why he would cheat. I look good, dress nice; I am a good mother and have sex with him on demand. I have a prosperous career and I carry my own weight, then to have him cheat on me with an overweight, poorly dressed raggedy heffa. Her nails weren't even done, and she wasn't wearing any jewelry."

Ms. Shirley took off her glasses and looked at me like I was speaking Greek.

"Baby, you know I'm old I didn't catch any of what you just said. Slow down girl and breathe. Now who did what with who? And got who some jewelry?"

That opened the floodgates, finally tearing up, I let it out. I cried uncontrollably for a few moments, frequently patting my tear-filled face with a napkin.

"Alicia, what's wrong I ain't never seen you so emotional."

"Ms. Shirley I found out yesterday that Arlington has been cheating on me. He denies that he slept with her and he's been apologizing but I don't believe him."

I began to tell Ms. Shirley about what happened. She got up from the table and started stirring her pot as she attentively nodded. She was one of the few people that had their dinner done before 3pm every day. After about ten minutes I was done with my spiel. I waited to hear what Ms. Shirley had to say because I knew she would tell me what I needed to do. Handing me a hanky out of the pocket of her duster and said,

"Here baby use this to wipe your face this is better than that rough napkin and stop that crying. Ooh wee, praise the Lord that you're finally finished. Child, did you hear what you just said? For the past ten minutes or so all I've heard is what YOU are. Not once did I hear you say what you are to him. Not once did I hear you say what he is to you or what ya'll are together. When you married that man *you* became *us, we,* and *our,* no longer *I.* Since you brought it up, I might as well go there."

Ms. Shirley took a deep breath, but her hand on her hip and continued.

"As long as I've known you, I ain't never seen you hug, kiss or show your husband any affection or appreciation. When Arlington walks in the door you give him some demand, question, or chore before saying hello or giving him a handshake. When was the last time you dated your husband? When was the last time you made love to your husband without him having to demand it? When was the last time you gave him a compliment or praise? Do you ask him or even care how his day was?"

My tears dried up immediately because I don't think Ms. Shirley heard anything I said,

"With all due respect Ms. Shirley I cannot give him what he don't ask for, that's his responsibility to tell me what his needs are. I ask for what I need and want. Why can't he do the same? Besides what in the world does that have to do with what I just said? Hello, he cheated on me. I didn't do anything wrong."

"I don't know what to say about the wives of today. Me and Mack, God rest his soul was married 35 years before the Lord called him home to glory. We were one. The Bible says that a man should leave his mother and father and cleave to his wife and the two shall become one."

As I listened to Ms. Shirley I was trying to figure out the relevancy of what she was saying. She and Mack had nothing to do with Arlington and me. But she kept on talking,

"You ladies today, ya'll always running around singing the *"I" song. I cook, I clean, I do this, I do that always I, I,* I. Hell, you are supposed to do those things. But you never utter us, him or us. If you got it all together, why be bothered with a husband at all? You wanna mistreat your husband, and then act like a mad attack dog when you think another woman is interested in him, or if you think his eyes are wandering. You act like you don't want him but you don't want anyone else to have him either. Whatever happened to us, we, or our when other women aren't around?

Do you even know what turns Arlington on? Do you know what excites him? Personally, I don't think you are mad at him for cheating, I think your pride is hurt because you have made it up in your mind that you are better than this other woman but she has your husband's attention. You need to read Proverbs 31. The woman brings the increase. You are simply doing what God ordained women to do which is to fulfill the physical needs of her husband."

I could tell Ms. Shirley was a little irritated at this point because she never broke her pace stirring her pot. I am the one that was dogged out so why is she upset with me? I had to ask,

"I don't understand why people always say the wife must be doing something wrong if her husband cheats, why can't it be that he's just a dog? Hell, when I don't get what I want I don't latch onto the first dick that comes swinging my way."

"I know you're mad, but don't forget who you're talking to lil girl." Ms. Shirley said with both hands on her hips.

"I'm sorry Ms. Shirley, I got carried away. I'm just mad that people always give the married man that cheats a pass."

"I can accept your apology, but can you accept the answer to your question?"

I sat back in my chair listening as Ms. Shirley adamantly continued,

"Arlington works hard, pays all the bills, and fathers his kids. He does whatever you ask him, he supports you, he encourages you, and what do you give him other than a foul attitude? He sends you flowers just because, YOU don't want for a damn thing. You take without giving, so you tell me who is the dog? Lucky for you I'm saved or else I would really tell you about yourself. Alicia, you got a good man. You better thank God for him."

I couldn't believe her, how dare she take his side? It has been 10 years since Mack died. I guess Ms. Shirley believes any man at this point is better than no man.

"Good, what is your definition of good? He only does those things because he wants sex. He doesn't genuinely mean anything he does. After all, how could he when he's had Piper for who knows for how long? Doing who knows what with her. Who knows how many other women he's cheated with, this is just the first time he got caught. Apparently, Ms. Shirley you don't understand what is going on. Things have changed from the way they were back in your day."

"Some things never change. A man still needs to feel like a man. You should treat your man like you do your children, but not as a child. A man needs love, attention, affection, and praise. The man said he didn't sleep with her. Why can't you accept that and find out what exactly was he getting from her. Attention, affection, praise maybe? How can you fight for your man when you don't know what you are up against? I know I'm on the outside looking in but from what I can see, you don't need, want, or desire anything. Rather than arguing with me, you should be asking yourself what was this woman's intent behind saying what she said to you."

"Ms. Shirley if he doesn't feel like a man already that is his self-esteem issue and I can't help him with that. I just know he slept with her, and as far as I am concerned there is never an excuse for cheating. That lets me know he lacks integrity and cannot be trusted. And, I need a man that I can trust. So I guess I don't have everything that I need."

Ms. Shirley sat down at the table with me and grabbed both of my hands.

"Did you ask Arlington to tell you what is going on with him and this girl? Just a thought but, just maybe she's lying to get your man, maybe this woman makes him feel good about himself, or just maybe you only see what you want to see. Honey shouldn't nobody be able to tell you anything about your husband. Baby, men aren't smart enough not get caught cheating. They are creatures of habit, if he is cheating believe me signs are there. Either he's not cheating or you aren't paying attention to the signs. Either way you gotta get YOU together."

"No, I didn't bother asking him anything because Piper told me everything I needed to hear. Besides if some tacky woman boosts his ego, then I can't do anything about it. But I guess when you live in the gutter garbage tastes good to you. I'm gonna let him stay in the gutter with her trifling ass. Pay attention? I ain't got the time. I have more things to worry about than babysitting a grown man to make sure he's doing what he said he would do, which is to love, honor, and respect till death do us part."

"Why you gotta be so nasty? Tell me why this woman gotta be garbage? Do you know anything about her?"

I hated to be rude but there was nothing else I needed to hear from Ms. Shirley. If I don't leave, I will cuss her out too. I grabbed my purse and dotted towards the door as Ms. Shirley mumbled,

"Maybe if you gave your husband some attention from time to time he wouldn't have to bribe you for sex. When you are ready to hear the truth you are welcomed to come back."

I rolled my eyes and slammed the door behind me. I was not in the mood to hear that backwoods, country, submissive, religious crap. I could not believe what just happened. I will not take responsibility because my husband chose to creep.

I aimlessly drove around for a couple hours. Arlington finally woke up and realized I was gone. He continuously called and sent me text messages. I refused to reply to his messages or return his calls. I was not ready to hear any of his bullshit or justification for his indiscretions. I can't help but wonder what would have happened if we hadn't bumped into this woman? How long would he have continued with his affair?

I found myself at Myra's doorstep. I joined her on the porch swing. She had the most tranquil house. The tulips in her yard seemed to always bloom full, beautiful and in perfect form. The majestic mountains in the distance were a breathtaking backdrop. My soul began to outpour. I was embarrassed that my perfect life lacked a perfect husband. Myra continued to rock silently and watched me cry until my tears disappeared into simple sobbing.

"Myra, I have invested too much into this marriage to just let it go and I be damned if I let a raggedy heffa destroy everything I built. Everywhere I go somebody's checking me out. Arlington should feel lucky that I am with him."

Myra sipped her iced tea in silence. But I was ready to hear what the "Lord" had to say. Whenever my sister opened her mouth, the words *God gave me this to give to you" always fell out of it.*

"Alicia, you are a strong, successful, independent woman. The Bible says that you are supposed to submit unto your husband as unto the Lord and Proverbs 31 speaks of a virtuous woman. Can you look in the mirror and a virtuous woman is reflected back at you? Did God tell you that Arlington was your husband? Have you gone to God in prayer about the situation?"

Boy, Myra can be a real mood killer. She gives compliments to boost you into the clouds just as you start soaring, she knocks you back to earth with an underhanded comment. I should have known she was baiting me in for the kill when she complimented me.

"You know Myra you are the second person today that has tried to feed me that Proverbs 31 crap. I know all about Proverbs 31, but what about the part in the Bible where it says follow your husband as he follows Christ? Since he isn't following Christ then that means I am casting my pearls before swine and the Bible, your Bible says don't do that. See I listen when I go to church. I have been faithful to my husband. He has everything he needs, even if he was unhappy that did not give him the right to cheat. The owness is on him, not me.

Besides how can you tell me anything when you don't even have a man?"

Myra sighed and shook her head.

"The Bible says two shall bare witness. Honey, this is your confirmation from the Lord that you need to seek Him, and He will direct your path. And, let's be clear, I don't have a man because I am happy living saved, satisfied, and single. The Lord is preparing me for my mate. But we are talking about you not me. You are the one hurting and showed up on my doorstep. Are you really giving Arlington what he needs or are you giving him what you think he should have?"

"You got to be kidding me. Don't blame Jesus because you can't keep yourself together long enough to catch a man's attention. Yes, I know Arlington is my husband, we're married aren't we? Therefore, I know what he needs."

I couldn't believe what she was trying to make me swallow. I looked at Myra with disgust as I walked off her porch. Before I reached the last step Myra shouted,

"You said you have worked too hard for what you have; I suggest you fight just as hard to keep it. Control your emotions long enough to listen to the voice of the Lord and He will tell you what to do about Arlington."

"Myra, there it goes! Your jealousy is rearing its ugly head again. Don't be jealous because I know what I want and refuse to settle for anything less. You been single so long, that you don't know what you should or shouldn't have to put up with. Keep seeking the voice of God, while I keep seeking the truth."

"Wow Alicia! Let that be the reason. You are wrong! The word of the Lord declares, I am the way the truth and the light, so the truth is in God. Keep ignoring sound advice and your husband if you want to. I'm just saying if he is cheating, you are giving him time to do it. The Bible says that the devil is roaming the earth to and fro seeking whom he may devour. Simply put he is looking for the opportunity to create chaos. You're giving Arlington the opportunity to cheat. I'll keep you lifted up in prayer; hope to see you at church tomorrow."

I kept walking. Myra can keep feeding herself that mess, but the last time I checked God was not dropping men out of heaven, nor was he delivering men to the doorstep of a no makeup wearing, Bible toting, recluse. This just wasn't my day and it was not even 10a.m. yet.

I usually run around with the kids on Saturdays, but my mom called and said they wanted to stay another night. I was thankful for that because I was not ready to play Holly Homemaker.

I found myself wandering through the mall. For the life of me, I don't even remember driving here or what I came to look at, but I am here. After walking in and out a few stores looking at everything and browsing for nothing, Cassie called and asked if I wanted to meet her for a late lunch.

After being beat up all morning, I knew it was safe to go with her. Cassie was always good for a laugh, and she didn't give a brotha no slack. I know she would understand and support me. Cassie and I decided to meet at a restaurant near the mall to save time. Ok, the truth was we decided to meet somewhere that had great martinis. I told Cassie what my life had been like over the last 24-hour hours. Laughing she said,

"You know this is why men today aren't worth two tears in a bucket. Men are only as faithful as opportunity. As long as there is no opportunity, a man will be faithful. Men are sorry and full of excuses. Because of "the man" they can't get a job. Because their wife isn't freaky, they cheat.

Because their father wasn't there, they never learned about commitment, because, because, because. But no one ever makes excuses for women. We birth nations, breed success, and bury failure. Yet we don't get a pass or be excused when we're sick or tired. We don't get to cat around town because we're stressed. However, men can walk over women, walk off their jobs, walk out on their responsibilities, walk down memory lane, and walk up like nothing is wrong. Hell, they should be tired of walking and sit the hell down somewhere. You damn right to make him suffer; I would make Arlington pay out the ass. By the time I finished with him, he would wish he wasn't born."

I could not agree with her more. I raised my glass for a toast,

"Amen, Cassie that is why you're my friend. You keeps it real."

"Hey, I'm just calling it like it is."

"You know Cassie the crazy part about this whole situation is because HE is suffering, we have to make up. Because HE loves me, HE wants to straighten this out, but what about me? I will never be able to trust him again. So what, if I don't make dinner one night or go a couple of days without giving him a lil sumthin, sumthin, will he go running to the nearest thing that got her legs gapped open?"

"If I were you, I would make Arlington suffer so much that he would rather sell his soul to the devil and burn in hell than even consider cheating on you again. I wouldn't divorce him though. He does pay the bills and he is a great piece of eye candy."

Cassie said with a chuckle. I couldn't agree with her more. Cassie and I continued talking about how disgusting men were. I was puzzled, men always talk about wanting a dime piece, a total package, but when the perfect ten walks into his life, they have no clue on what to do with a good woman. He always thinks there is something better and winds up with someone who's not worth change for a nickel in found pennies.

"Cassie, since it is me and you talking, let me tell you what pisses me off the most. This Piper girl's hair looked a hot mess. She's about a size 14, carrying a sad excuse of a bag and she was too raggedy to even wear earrings. If he had to cheat, he could have cheated with someone that was at least on my level. I said it once, and I will say it again, when men spend time in the gutter, they think garbage tastes good. He got a Mercedes but would rather drive that Pinto."

"You ain't said nothing but a word, then ya'll wonder why I am single. I am single because I enjoy my peace of mind, I got everything I want. I come and go as I please. Because I am not committed to no one, no one feels obligated to lie to me. You got to understand men are hunters and once they conquer, they lose interest. For them the fun is in the chase not the capture."

See Cassie was my true friend. She was not going to let me take the blame because my husband was raggedy. Cassie continued,

"This is why I got girlfriends, I can sit, eat, drink, laugh, male-bash non-stop, and then go get DBD. And we all know what DBD is Dick By Default," we said in unison.

"It ain't from who we want, but it is what we want." Cassie and I gave each other a high-five across the table, as we chuckled joyfully.

"Alicia do you remember that guy I was dating DJ?"

"Boy do I. That brotha looked like DAMN! That was the only way I can describe him."

"Yes Alicia that's the one. His alluring smile would seduce the prudest of women. His cologne could reduce the proudest of women. He had the body of an Arabesque Man of the month. Let's not forget those silky dreadlocks that outlined his smooth, dark chocolate face and fell just above his broad strong shoulders, and that swagger. Whoa! Girl let me quit, I got sidetracked."

With a sigh, Cassie and I raised our glasses to each other again.

"I ain't mad. DJ is so fine he could sidetrack a compass. What's up with him though?"

"Why all of a sudden he got feelings for a sista?"

"You got to be kidding me. *Mr. I am the best thing since sliced bread. Mr. you should be proud I graced you with a one night stand* got feelings for someone other than himself?"

"Girl yeah!"

"What are you gonna do?"

"Absolutely nothing! Like I always say, men love the chase and like the capture. I'm going to enjoy being courted. I am going to let him wine, dine, and if I think about it long enough, I might let him 69 me. You know how I do. But the only reason he wants me is because I don't worship the ground that he walks on like all the other women he knows."

"Cassie you are my hero."

"Girl, I just do what I do. All women need to understand, men are supposed to keep us laid and paid. Love is not part of the equation; it only equates to heartbreak. Men value what they pay for. The more it costs the more they love until the latest, greatest, new generation model shows up."

I should have adopted Cassie's mindset before I caught up with Arlington. Cassie was living her life without all the drama. She had her own money, she called her own shots, and men were flocking at her feet. I needed to know what my next move should be.

"So tell me, what do you know about this chick Arlington is messing with?"

"The only thing I know is that her name is Piper Middleton."

"Even though you are making Arlington pay out the ass, we still need to teach that Piper hoe a lesson. She should be ashamed of herself throwing her ass at a married man. I gotta hand it to you, if she would have said to me what she said to you, her fronts would be gone. She would be picking teeth off the concrete."

"The situation caught me so off guard that I didn't know what the hell to do. But I promise, if I ever see her again, lawd help me. I wonder what I can get out the kids about her?"

"Alicia, it's time for you to put that high class attitude aside and get dirty! Men aren't that smart. I promise if you do just a little searching you will be able to find out everything you want to know about her. Denver ain't that big."

"I think I can do without the details of her and my husband's escapades."

"I will track down Piper, disrupt her life. Put her on spook. I plan to torment the hell outta her."

"Ok, I will let you know what I find."

"I promise I wish we would run into her just one time. I want to cuss her out just one good time for you. As soon as I get home, I'll Google her."

"Thanks girl, I'm glad you understand and not cram *God* down my throat. I'm still mad at Myra's ignorant ass."

"Alicia, I'm mad at you for talking to somebody that ain't never had a man about your man. What did you expect her to say? She has no reference point. She only knows what comes across the pulpit on Sunday mornings. Which we all know ain't nothing but a bunch of emotional hype. You know I love God, but He gave us five senses for a reason. You worry about Arlington and I will handle Piper."

"You got it. I hope his bank account can cover his indiscretion check. The way I look at it is, he's been buying dinners, movies, flowers, maybe giving up a little gas change to his hoe for the past year and that money came out of my household so he got to give me that money back with interest. Hoe notes are expensive in more ways than one."

"Look at you Alicia. That is what I'm talking about. If you don't mean nothing to him, I bet his money sure in the hell does."

"I'm a quick study girl. I spent too much effort molding him into the man I wanted him to be, to lose him to a woman that can obtain or maintain him. Quiet as it's kept, he can't maintain himself."

I admired Cassie so much. She was always sure of herself and firmly stood her ground. At the end of the day, I knew Cassie had my back if no one else did. For about another hour or so, Cassie and I laughed and enjoyed our sista friend time. This was exactly what I needed, an arena to blow off some steam.

This Castle Ain't Home

I walked in the door to find the house dimly lit by candlelight, the Greatest Slow Jams of All Times was playing softly, and there were red rose petals sprinkled across a white comforter that was laid in front of the fireplace. A bottle of wine was chilling on the coffee table with two glasses set up. I pray Arlington didn't have the audacity to have that raggedy ass Piper in my house. I promise somebody is headed to hell and somebody will be going to jail tonight, if this trifling brotha was romancing his hoe in my damn house.

I noticed Arlington at the top of the stairs. Either he was looking damn good or I had too many martinis. He was wearing his black silk pajama pants and a white wife beater, showing off his chocolate sculptured shoulders and smooth, chiseled chest. He was not playing fair. He even had on his "come get me cologne."

"Welcome home baby, I've been waiting for you." Arlington said as he slowly began to walk down the staircase. I was mesmerized, he knew exactly how to catch my attention. Cassie's words began to ring through, "make him pay out the ass."

I hope he doesn't think making up would be this easy. If I wave the white flag now, he will never learn his lesson. I waited until he got to the bottom of the stairs. I silently made a beeline past him, up the stairs, straight to the master bathroom. I walked like I hadn't noticed a thing, only to walk into the bathroom illuminated by candles a full tub of water, topped with bubbles and rose petals. I would have fell for the okey doke, but Cassie's words were still ringing through my head. Her words kept me strong. Out of the master bedroom here comes Arlington.

"Alicia, if you don't want to talk, at least listen to me."

I rolled my eyes and turned away like he hadn't said nothing. I can't believe he thought I would forgive him if he threw himself at me. Hell it's only been 24 hours and he's acting like I'm mad because he forgot to take out the trash or something.

"Ok, I'm done trying, I'll clean things up downstairs and sleep in my man cave tonight, but understand I pay the bills up in here, so I will not be inconvenienced. I will be sleeping in my bed tomorrow night with or without you."

"You ain't running nothing but your mouth, if it wasn't for me, you wouldn't have money to pay the bills."

"Since you want to play that card, let the truth be told, if you wasn't pregnant with AJ, I would have never married you, and I wouldn't be going through this. I was man enough to lay up with you, so I had to be man enough to stand up and accept responsibility for my actions."

I turned my back to Arlington, snatching the comforter over my head. I couldn't believe that he just said that. He was just being hurtful for no reason. Everyone knows I am the best thing that ever happened to him.

The next morning, I moved out of our bedroom and was sleeping in the guest room. I avoided Arlington as much as possible, only speaking to him when it was absolutely necessary. Avoiding conversation of any kind was the only way to ensure that an argument wouldn't develop.

I managed to keep the silent treatment up for weeks. I made sure I held my tongue especially when the children were around. I didn't want them to hear us arguing and think we were mad at them. It was hard to hold my peace because I really wanted to give Arlington a piece of my mind. Every now and then I had to call Cassie for a pep talk because Arlington was looking good and I was feeling a little sorry for making him suffer, but I stood my ground. I called Cassie with an update.

"Cassie the silent treatment is working. Arlington has been sending me flowers every other day, been inviting me on dates, sending apologetic emails and everything."

"You go girl. Stick to your guns and stick it to him. Keep telling him no, and I would not answer his phone calls every now and then so he don't think that you are just sitting around waiting for him. Hell, make him think that you are out with another man."

"Thanks for the pep talk because I do want to give him some. You know make up sex is always the bomb."

"I hear you girl but he has to really learn his lesson. Well, let me get back to work. I'll check in with you tomorrow. Text me if you need something in the meantime." I was so glad that I had a friend like Cassie, a true friend that supported and understood me.

One evening Arlington caught me alone in the laundry room, up until this point I managed to never be caught alone with him. I took all precautions, I made sure one of the kids slept in bed with us a few nights a week, I left before he woke up, I came home after he went to sleep. I was not trying to hear nothing he had to say.

"You can't keep acting like this. I know you are hurt, and I am sorry about that. I miss you and I am suffering without you. Come on Alicia, it's been weeks, the silent treatment has gone on long enough. Can we talk and try to work this out, let's go get counseling, talk to Pastor or something. Our marriage, our family is important to me."

Perplexed I looked at him and asked,

"You created this situation not me, so why should I be concerned that you are suffering? You should have thought about the consequences of your actions before you did the act. You should have thought about our family before you threw it away for an orgasm. I hope it was the best nut you ever had."

"You got the relationship with me, and Piper twisted. I keep telling you we never had sex. Listen, me and Piper usually talk about twice a week, and I see her once a week during basketball season. I had lunch with her once to thank her for helping me with the kids and as I already told you, I only went to her house that one time. But, what I can say she gave me the attention when you wouldn't."

"See that's exactly what I was talking about, you and your low ass self-esteem. I can't help it if you aren't secure in your manhood. Hell, man your punk ass up. You wouldn't be shit if I didn't pick you up out the gutter and dust your raggedy ass off."

"I understand that you are mad, but there is no reason for you to be ignorant. I ain't gonna argue with you and I'll be damned if I stand here and let you attack my manhood. Sorry or not you wanted me, so what exactly does that say about you? You was not and are not my savior. I was happy with the life I was living before I married you. I had a drama-free life."

I was appalled that he would talk to me like that. He should be grateful that someone took interest in him. I guess my face said it all.

"Oh, now you quiet. I didn't think you would have a response to that. I have to go to Phoenix for a week and I was trying to make things right between us before I left but I guess you have already made up your mind that you don't want to get back on track."

"See I knew it was a trick to all this. I guess since I didn't screw you, Piper is gonna meet you in Phoenix for a rendezvous. This is exactly why I don't trust you."

"Alicia, I told you a million times. I did not sleep with her. You haven't even let me explain the situation to you. I keep telling you, we never had sex, but you are too ignorant to hear me. I ain't now nor have I ever been her man. I will call her and prove it to you. If you aren't willing to work this out, then what, do you want a divorce? I have tried everything I know how to do to prove to you I love you, I regret that I befriended Piper and I am sorry for hurting you."

"Oh, you want to take the easy way out. You want me to tell you I want a divorce so you can use that as an excuse of why you walked out on your family for another woman. I won't do your dirty work for you. If you want a divorce then by all means file."

"You win. You can't ever say I didn't try. Good night."

I guess we didn't have anything else to talk about; I damn sure wasn't interested in nothing that he had to say. I knew this was a plot. If he would have pushed a little harder, I would have gave him some, but I guess he's saving it for his "business trip."

I went about my merry little way, jumped in the shower and took my happy ass to bed. I awoke the next morning to find Arlington gone. I couldn't believe he really left, I had to call Cassie and tell her what was going on.

"Cassie girl, are you at work yet?"

"No ma'am this is spa day for me. What's up?"

"Ok, why did Arlington tell me last night that he is headed to Phoenix for a week on business? And, he left this morning before I woke up."

"He just told you last night and was up and gone before you woke up! Oh hell no. I bet you a nail to a nickel that sorry bastard is laid up with his raggedy hoe somewhere. If I was you, I would pack that fool's shit, drop it off at his father's house and change the locks. If he wants to go back to living in the gutter let him."

"Myra and Ms. Shirley have been like, Alicia give him a chance, you should listen to what he has to say, forgive him and move on."

"No, hell no. He don't give a damn about you. Forgive him if you want to and I will be calling you Lucy Lunchmeat."

"I think I'm gonna pack up the kids and move out. I would rather pay rent and storage somewhere and let him worry about the bills over here."

"You're damn straight, and I bet Piper can't keep house and got a bunch kids too."

"Alright, girl let me get my day started."

"Alicia, call me if you need me."

After dropping the kids off at school for the day, I began my search for movers and a place to stay. I was determined to be gone before he got back. Arlington was going to pay for what he did and is doing to our family. I was gonna make sure that he thought about it twice before he considered cheating on me again and in order to do that, he is gonna have to know and feel what it is like not to have me around.

I guess I just need to face the fact that I am too much woman for him. He needs someone that ain't nothing so he could feel better about himself, I bet Piper won't be able to maintain what I obtained because she don't understand the cost. I'm just gonna get a three bedroom apartment, condo or something.

I found a place that I liked immediately, and the movers were scheduled to be here two days later. My plan was moving along without a single hitch. As my momma always say *Jesus will work it out*. The movers arrived. I had them pack up and move everything but Arlington's clothes and everything in his man cave. He should be grateful that I am leaving the home entertainment center and his clothes. I should have thrown all his stuff away, let that hoe buy his clothes and wash his drawls.

The kids and I were all settled in our new place. I told them that we were on vacation while their dad was traveling for his job. I didn't have the heart to tell the kids that their father chose a piece of ass over them. Exactly seven days later almost to the minute, my cell phone rang.

"Alicia what in the hell is going on? I just got back from Phoenix where are you and my kids? Where is all our furniture and stuff?"

I don't understand why Arlington is upset. He abandoned our marriage. I simply did what he did; I took my blocks and left the playground. I don't know why he thought he could go lay up for a week and come home like nothing ever happened.

"Me, my kids, and the furniture I picked out have moved on with our lives. Now you don't have to sneak or pretend, you can go ahead and be with your boo. I already know you were laid up somewhere. Cassie was right, she told me not to forgive you."

"Alicia, you have access to every aspect of my life, you can find out where I been if you wanted to. I may be a lot of things, and you should know me well enough to know that a liar ain't one of them. But damn what do I gotta to say? Your problem ain't with me; it is you. You keep listening to your manless, dumb ass friends. How are you gonna take advice from a chick that can't get or keep a man? It puzzles the hell out of me why you can talk to everybody but me about our relationship? When you start asking your friends what they think because you are looking for somebody to support what you're feeling, not because you are looking for answers. You are listening to what makes you feel good about your actions. That so-called advice from your friends usually includes some type of vengeance. Now a really good friend will give you supportive truth no matter how painful, to resolve things without bashing or ganging up on your man."

I'm mad Arlington thinks our marriage is on the rocks because of my friends. My friends have nothing to do with the fact that he got caught cheating. But I'll be damned if I sit here and let him talk about my girls. They always got my back, so I damn sure got theirs.

"Don't hate! Cassie don't have a man because she rather be free than deal with a man and his lies like I'm doing now. You are just intimidated by me, Cassie or any other strong, independent black woman."

"Why would I ever be intimidated by a lonely ass trick? If there is something wrong with every man she meets, the common denominator is her. She needs to check herself. Cassie needs to spend six months tending to her business and another six months staying out of our business. If you feel we can't talk about us, then our relationship is already destroyed. Communication is the smallest element of a relationship, but a relationship can't survive without it. If you were looking for answers rather than allies you would have gotten wisdom from your momma, Ms. Shirley or somebody with some damn sense. I'm tired of trying; we will do this your way."

"Save it Arlington, you wouldn't be shit if it wasn't for me. I made you what you are. You were a functioning alcoholic, moving from job to job, even with a roommate you were struggling to keep your head above water, making just enough money to keep from being homeless until I married your sorry ass. Even though my friends told me not to marry you, I did anyway."

"Since you want to go there, let's go. You are absolutely right. I am what I am today because of you. I only fucked you because I was drunk. A drunk linked me to you forever. I've done a bunch of shit in my life that I'm not proud of but screwing you is the only thing I regret. I knew you weren't capable of being anything more than a bootie call, but because I was too drunk to put on a condom, I got stuck with you. I only married because you were knocked up and it was cheaper than giving you 35% of my paper for you to piss off on your hair and nails. After we got married, I woke up every day telling myself that I love you until I finally started to believe it. Every time I think about getting drunk, I think about how much my last drink cost me. I lost my true love, to be with a woman that doesn't appreciate me. I can't win for losing with you. You win, if it doesn't have to do with my kids, you won't ever hear from me again."

"See there you go trying to blame me because of your insecurities. Go ahead play house with Piper, while she think she's getting you, I hope she knows you are coming with an ex-wife and babies. I'm a woman about mines, Piper needs to be a woman about hers and face me. She been laying up with you for more than a year, so I'm sure she knows where to find me if she got something that she needs to say to me."

"Piper ain't our problem, like I said, your stupid ass friends in your ear is our damn problem. You, Myra, and Cassie will be some lonely ass, has been hoes, sitting in a dusty house with each other, a cat, wishing you had somebody to love you. You don't know anything about Piper so you should keep her name out your mouth. I'm not dealing with your ignorance today. I'm getting my kids this weekend. I'll holla at you then."

Arlington made his demand and hung up on me. Who does he think he is? Why did he feel the need to defend Piper? I had to call Cassie.

"Guess who finally surfaced from their week long rendezvous with an attitude?"

"What the hell he got an attitude for? He been laid up for a week, he should be nothing but giggles and grins!"

"Cassie, listen to this BS, he misses his kids, he loves me, and telling me I don't know nothing about Piper blah, blah, blah."

"I'm so glad you moved out, I bet Piper ain't as attractive once he came home to a cold stove and empty house. Damn him, you are a strong, independent, black woman, and you don't need a man."

I was hyped up now and feeling good about myself. Arlington needed me, I didn't need him. I got this.

"Well, girl let me get off the phone. Without Arlington here, you know I'm a taxi cab now. Speaking of which will you be able to pick up Ariah from gymnastics for me at 8:00 tonight and bring her home?"

"I wish I could, but tonight I'm meeting this guy for dinner. But you can count on me any other time."

"Alright, girl holla at me tomorrow."

I knew everything Cassie was saying was right. The fact that Arlington was pursuing me so passionately let me know that he was still in love with me. That meant I had him just where I wanted him. Everything was moving just like Cassie had predicted. I just wished I was as strong as she was.

I don't think I can keep up this charade much longer. I desired to be with my husband. And, I don't know how far I could push him without him breaking. That last conversation got me a little worried. He has never said such vicious things like that to me before.

Life without Arlington around left me feeling like I was dead inside and I was just going through the motions of life as if I was a synchronized robot. Nothing really mattered to me. I just could not understand why Arlington would throw our marriage out the window. I know I was the one that moved out, but it was up to him to win me back. Up to this point, I can say that I am convinced that he loves me and would rather die than cheat again.

Cassie and Myra said they had my back, but it seemed like whenever I needed them to help with the kids, they were always busy. I even stopped getting invitations to our girl's night out events. It's been a while since I had a martini or ate at a grown people restaurant. I think if I even see another chicken finger, I will start clucking.

My parents helped as much as they could, but they lived the life of a retired couple. It seemed like they were on vacation more than they were at home. Being a single parent is hell. The kids were even starting to get on my nerves. Every time I took them somewhere or did anything with them, I had to hear, daddy does this, daddy takes us there, daddy this, daddy that, daddy, daddy, daddy. I'm mad he got my kids thinking his sorry ass is all that.

Although, I walked around with a smile on my face, I was torn up inside but my pride had the best of me. Sleeping alone at night was not cute. At night when the house was still and quiet my mind would race about all of what I thought Arlington was doing or could be doing in our home.

I periodically would call him late at night to see exactly what he was doing. I would camouflage the calls with something trivial about the kids. But like Cassie said, I have to stick to my guns. To make the situation worse, this single parent thing is not working with me. I should take Arlington back for no other reason but to help me take care of these kids. He still took AJ to practice but after a long day at the office, I still had to make a variety of stops, come home, cook, clean and bathe the children.

This was more than what I signed up for. I loved being a mother, but I felt like I didn't have a life. All I did was work and take care of the kids. I can't remember the last time I had some "me" time.

I have been working 12-hour days trying to get this deliverable together for a major client that I was trying to sign. Ms. Shirley was able to help me out by babysitting, but I really needed someone to run around for me but Ms. Shirley never learned to drive.

I walked into Ms. Shirley's back door one evening to pick up Ariah. It looked like she was cleaning up after her. AJ was with Arlington, he usually stayed the night with his father on the evenings that he had football practice.

"Hey, Ms. Shirley, where is Ariah?" I asked as I plopped down in a chair at the kitchen table. "Look what the cat drug in, she just finished eating a snack now she's glued to the television set. I want to know, how long do you plan to carry on like this?"

"What are you talking about?"

"Alicia you look like death warmed over."

"I thought I looked cute in my Anne Klein suit."

"You do look good in your suit, but baby I'm looking into your eyes. I see such sorrow, and then to compound it, you look plain exhausted."

Ms. Shirley said as she continued wiping down the counter.

"I'm just focused on this project that I am working on that is why I look tired."

Ms. Shirley folded her dish towel and laid it on the sink before she came and sat at the table. That usually meant that I was about to get a lecture. Lord knows today was not the day, but I had to suck it up anyhow after all she was the only help, I had with the kids.

"Alicia, who do you think you are foolin? Neither women nor men were meant to do this alone. Men provide and protect while women love, support and nurture. You are on the run from 6 in the morning until at least 8 at night because you are stubborn. Because you are so hell bent on being right and making Arlington suffer, that you are killing yourself. Look at you, how much weight have you lost because you are so stressed and not eating right? You have every right to be angry at Arlington if he cheated, but you don't even know why you're mad, you are just trying to prove a point."

"You and I have already had this conversation. And, I refuse to rehash it again. It's clear that you and I don't see eye to eye on this subject. Just let it go."

"Child, I am only telling you this because I love you. The kids see you, but don't spend time with you because you are either coming or going. You can do whatcha want to do, all I'm saying is, if you have made up your mind that your marriage is over then end it. That way you both can move on. Right is not always good or best. Remember, emotions lie, so I reckon you should pay attention to reason."

Everything Ms. Shirley said made sense. I still loved Arlington and I missed him like crazy, but a man can fix everything but his broken word. I want him to hurt and suffer like he made me hurt and suffer. How would I ever learn to trust him again? I gathered my daughter, her things and said goodbye to Ms. Shirley. As I was walking out the door she said,

"God doesn't put more on us than we can bare, but what we put on ourselves will kill us." I just nodded my head. I was too tired to argue or respond.

After putting Ariah to bed, I decided to call Arlington before I went to sleep. Each time I dialed his number it rang directly to voicemail. I didn't bother leaving a message. I almost bought what Ms. Shirley was selling until I discovered that Arlington was so busy with his new boo that is why he couldn't answer the phone. And, he still got my child around his hoe. I wanted to go over and beat that heffa down. But, I knew there was no one to keep Ariah and I had an early morning. Ok, the truth of the matter is, I'm so worn out tonight that I would be an easy win.

The next morning Arlington came to pick up Ariah so they can spend a few days together. I'm glad he decided to take the kids because today was my big presentation day. I needed a little extra time to get dressed and trying to gather bags, backpacks, and kids would not get me in game mode.

Arlington usually called me to let me know that he was in front of the house and he waited in the car until the kids came out. This time he sent AJ to the door to let me know they were outside.

"AJ why did you come ring the doorbell instead of your dad calling?"

"Yesterday I was playing a game on daddy's phone and I dropped his phone and it broke. He is going to have to buy a new one today. I was sad, but daddy told me that mistakes happen and next time hold the phone tight like I hold a football."

I just smiled at AJ as he followed the Ariah out the door. I felt a little stupid because I convinced myself that Arlington was up to no good. Thank God he didn't know I tried to call. At least I saved myself some embarrassment by not having to apologize.

Just as I imagined, I knocked the client's socks off. It was an exceptionally hard day for me. I just closed the biggest deal of my career. After escorting my new clients out, I sat behind my desk. I was so excited and wanted to share my news with my best friend. I picked up the phone to dial Arlington's office. Whenever something good or bad happened, he was always the first person I called. It finally dawned on me that Arlington was my best friend and he wasn't around for me to share my news. I knew if I couldn't depend on no one else I knew that I could depend on Arlington to be happy for me and with me. He even would buy me a gag gift. One year, he bought me a Mr. Potato Head after I got a promotion because I was ahead of the competition.

I was sad that I couldn't call my best friend but, I can't sweat the small stuff. I am a strong, independent, black woman. If I closed this deal alone, surely I could celebrate alone.

Let the Game Begin

Since the children were with Arlington I decided to take a well-deserved, long overdue "me day." This was the perfect time for me to get a massage, wax, pedicure, manicure, and a new hairdo. After spending more than six hours at the spa, went home to get dressed. I needed a new attitude to match my new look. I slide on a long, sexy summer dress, accented with nothing more than my Gucci shades and open toed sandals.

I took my truck in to have it detailed just as an excuse to cruise around the city. I knew I still had it going on because I turned heads everywhere I went. All of the attention reminded me that I did not need a man in my life, I was all I needed, but it felt good to have my ego stroked and be complimented by men. I was feeling good about me, the hell with that no good, cheating, sorry excuse of a husband.

Arlington might have had passion with Piper, but I gave him purpose. If he couldn't recognize the diamond he had, then he deserved that lump of coal that he called Piper. I wish Arlington realized coal gives heat and eventually burns up, but diamonds are strong and last forever.

I had to finally end my day away from reality, free from the office, house, husband, and kids. I decided to stop for coffee before heading home for the evening. I patiently waited as the clerk finished freshly grinding, only I turn around to see

"Ms. Piper" walking through the heading towards me. She had the gall to smile at me and say hello. I rolled my eyes and said,

"You don't know me nor do you have the right to speak to me." I kept my pace towards the door. I could not let this moment pass. I needed to give this woman a piece of my mind. I turned back around and invited Piper to join me for a woman to woman powwow. Surprisingly she was more than willing to oblige me. I didn't think she would be woman enough to face me. After she got her coffee, she sat at the table with me. Before Piper could get all the way positioned in her seat, I started right in,

"I am so sick of you trifling ass women that can't get a man of your own always going after someone else's husband. Do you really think he would leave a woman like me for someone like you? The same way you catch him, will be the way that you lose him. If he cheated on me with you, what makes you think he wouldn't cheat on you? I don't understand how you can even call yourself a woman and you are creeping with someone else's husband. You are going to burn in hell. I am surprised that you are willing to go to hell for nothing more than a wet belly because I know he ain't paying for your raggedy ass." I blurted.

Piper sat back in her chair, shook her head and said,

"Are you done? Because you got life and bullshit mixed up for real. Let me introduce you to reality. I met your husband at a basketball game 18 months or so ago. My brother referees in Arlington's basketball league. Periodically, I go watch the games because I love basketball and to support my brother. Your kids were at the game one evening. I noticed that they were bored and restless, so I decided to take them to the concession stand for snacks. Then, I pulled some highlighters and stuff out of my bag and let them color."

Piper continued,

"When the game was over Arlington introduced himself to me and thanked me for helping him with the kids. After a few weeks of hanging out with the kids while Arlington played basketball, he asked could he take me to lunch to thank me. Apparently, you weren't interested in sharing in that aspect of his life."

I think she just threw a jab on the low low. I could not believe this woman was actually trying to justify being with my husband while insinuating I was neglecting him. So I interrupted,

"Piper you don't know what you are talking about I have Yoga on Wednesday's and the kids would rather go to their dad's basketball game. So don't try to tell me about my kids or think you know my husband."

Piper smirked,

"Oh, I can't tell you anything about your husband. Did you know he is the captain of his basketball team and his team set the league record two years in a row? Did you know he has been asked to take over the Western region? That is why he went to Phoenix to negotiate with another dealer about the agencies there. Did you know he was awarded Broker/Dealer of the year by Wall Street Power Movers? Do you know that?"

Wow, this chick really think she got one up on me, let me teach her a couple of things.

"Ok, you know a few trivial, common knowledge things about my husband whoop-de-doo! I guess hoes are worthy of a little pillow talk too. You don't know nothing more than any stranger can Google."

Piper leaned in towards me,

"I am a lady and you will respect me as such. I haven't called you out of your name; therefore you do not get to call me out of mine. Now that we got that clear let's continue."

I just looked at Piper like she was crazy. I'm going to let her have that one for grins.

"Ok Piper you got the floor. By all means tell me why you thought it was ok, to chase another woman's husband?"

"I'm not going to lie to you or anyone else. I'm in love with Arlington, and have been forever but he only views me as is a friend, a little sister of sorts. He has never been inappropriate with me. Let the truth be told, Arlington is not even capable of loving anyone as much as he loves you. For the last year I have had to pretend that I don't have feelings for him, when he confides in me and shares things with me that you refuse to hear. It hurts like hell to know that I am everything you're not, I have everything he needs, but all he desires is you."

I could not believe what I was hearing. This woman admits that she doesn't measure up to me, but actually thought she had a chance to hold the position that I held. At some point, she should have realized that things with my husband weren't going further than the bedroom. I felt sorry for her; she was tearing up and everything.

"Maybe now you will think twice before you toot your ass in the air for another married man."

"You still don't get it. Arlington and I have never had sex. We never even came close. You are so caught up in yourself that you didn't hear anything I just said. It's because of ungrateful, selfish women like you that I can't get a good man. God sent you a perfectly good man that provides for you, that loves you, that protects you, and faithful to you. And, you don't do anything but emasculate him, tear down his self-esteem, and kill his pride. See what pissess me off is when you are done with him, he won't be good for nobody. Because he has made a vow to never let another woman hurt him like that again. In order to protect himself he cuts off that part of his heart never to recovered or revisited again."

Piper's eyes began to tear up as she continued.

"Do you know how many times I ordered flowers for you from him, do you know many times I had to look at disappointment of his face because you missed an awards ceremony or failed to give him a well done? Do you know how many times I helped him pick out the "perfect gift" for you and all Arlington said to me was good looking out? I made up that story in the store because I knew it would set you off. You behaved exactly how I thought you would, giving me a chance with Arlington. I thought he would allow me to comfort him and have the opportunity to show him that I am a good woman worthy of more than being just a friend. However, it backfired on me because what I didn't count on is that Arlington's love for you was really as strong as he proclaimed it to be."

Piper picked the napkin up from the table and began to gently pat the tears that were rolling down her cheek.

"See Alicia, I thought with you out of the way that I would finally get my shot, instead I lost a friend. Arlington said I betrayed him, and he could never forgive me for hurting you. I could not believe him, you hurt him, but he was mad at me for hurting you. In some twisted way, that only made me love him more. Despite everything Arlington remained, loyal and in love with you, a woman that doesn't understand the value of the treasure that she has. A woman that can't see past her wants long enough to identify her husband's needs."

I was paralyzed. I could not believe what I was hearing. This was not the conversation that I was expecting to have with her. Piper took a deep breath, with a serious look on her face she began to speak.

"Let me share something with you woman to woman. I married my college sweetheart, had a daughter, and planned to live happily ever after. My life was perfect. I was a wife and a mother. During the first game of my husband's pro career, he blew out his knee, unable to ever play ball again. I became his punching bag; I became the target of all of his anger and regret. I didn't know how to support him. I couldn't know how to comfort him. I didn't understand his anger, guilt, and disappointment."

I just listened to her wondering where this story was going. I wish she noticed that I wasn't interested in nothing she had to say. I looked down at my watch as she kept talking.

"When my husband was in one of his moods, I would take my daughter and leave the house until I thought my husband had passed out drunk. One night, the baby and I came in later than what he thought we should, and he began beating me. Before I knew it, he grabbed his gun. I grabbed my daughter and ran towards the door without coats, shoes or my purse. I was holding my scared little girl so tight that she began to cry. He fired a single shot, I kept running. After less than 10 minutes of running, I found refuge at the nearby fire station."

"We were safe; we had escaped never to return again. It was then that I discovered as I ran, life was streaming from my little girl running down the front of my clothes. The firemen did all they could but, that single shot killed my little girl. Long story short, once my husband found out what he had done, he took his own life."

"Piper that is truly a sad story and I'm sorry about your little girl. But, stealing my husband won't take that pain away or bring any good to you."

"You don't get it; you are sitting there so smug. I didn't want your life or your husband; I desired a second chance, a chance to love, to be a wife. See I expected my husband to be perfect and provide me with a perfect life. I didn't realize perfection took work until, I lost it all in one night. Believe me there is nothing cute about having a big house and fat bank account and you are alone, all alone. I watched how Arlington loved you. I finally got to see what true love looked like. It was so close but out of my reach. Do you know how hard it is to pretend you're not in love? There were so many times I wished that Arlington would just give me a hug of comfort, rather than the one arm cordial hug he gives me."

I could not believe Piper was going in on me like this. I listened as she kept talking.

"Just so that you know since you moved out, Arlington has not spent time with another woman and has ceased all contact with me. He came to see me before you moved out and begged me to confront you and tell you the truth. Instead I tried to plead my case and he shot me down without hesitation. If you don't remember anything I say, remember that a perfect relationship takes work whether your mate is or isn't doing their part; you still have to do yours. Your husband is willing to work, are you?"

Without saying a word to Piper, I grabbed my purse and ran the door. I needed to go get my husband back. I worked too hard for the life I lived and I was not ready to give it up. Since I spent the day pampering myself, I thought it would be my perfect opportunity. I sent Arlington a text. *Will you take the kids to my parents and if you don't mind join me for dinner I'm coming to our house. It's time we talked.* Without hesitation Arlington agreed to let me come to the house.

After stopping by the store, I headed to our home. Walking into the house, it was exactly the way it was when I moved out of it months ago. I set up a candlelight dinner on the patio, I threw a couple of steaks and crab legs on the grill. I pulled out his favorite bottle of wine and turned the stereo on.

When Arlington walked in the house, I played it cool. I was wearing his favorite perfume and a long, black spaghetti strapped dress. My makeup was soft and flawless. I made sure I was giving off an alluring sexy understated look. Jackpot! The look on Arlington's face told the entire story. I didn't hug or kiss him. It was important that I maintained my cool.

"Arlington, dinner is almost done. Go on upstairs, shower and get comfortable. Then we can eat." Arlington paused for a brief moment and headed towards the staircase without saying a word. While he was upstairs, I put everything in its place.

After a quick shower Arlington returned to the kitchen, he came around the corner into the kitchen with his basketball shorts on, pulling a white tee over his bald head that wasn't completely dry. The scent of his cologne subdued the aroma of the grill. He knew damn well I love him in basketball shorts. Arlington was playing dirty by not putting the shirt on until I was in sight. Leaning on the granite-topped island I said,

"We have been separated for more than six months now, paying for two households, the kids have half their stuff in one place and the other half in another. I think we spend more time transporting them than we do with them. I'm here tonight to say I'm sorry. I want my friend back, I need my husband, and I got completely waxed today."

Arlington smiled at me as I continued,

"I have been acting like a spoiled brat and you didn't deserve it, better yet I don't deserve a man that loves me as much as you do. Let's start all over again. Let's go away, rent a beach front villa in Jamaica for a week and find where we lost each other. This whole thing is my fault. As much as I hate to say it, I was wrong."

"Alicia, thank you for coming home, I have been asking God every day to send you home. I have been praying that I get my family back. This isn't all your fault, even though I never slept with Piper being intimate with her was wrong. Thank you."

Arlington hugged me tightly and kissed me on the top of my head.

"I know you might think this is too soon, but can I please make love to my wife? Self-service is not what it's cracked up to be."

"What about dinner?"

"You are all that I have an appetite for."

Arlington pulled me in his arms, passionately kissing me. He lifted me onto the island and continued to kiss me. I forgot how good he felt. Those strong shoulders and chiseled arms were like no other place on earth. I was walking on sunshine. I had to pull away because things were getting hot.

"Let me at least put the food away, I plan to pull an all-nighter. I will grab the wine and bring it upstairs and meet you upstairs."

"Leave the food, leave everything, we can clean it up in the morning." Arlington said as he planted gentle pecks on my face, lips and neck.

"You say that now, but when you wake up in the morning wanting some grits, steak, and eggs you're gonna wish I had put the food away."

"That's for damn sure."

Arlington grabbed me by my waist and lifted off the kitchen island and lowered me back to my feet. He watched me attentively as I started putting away the food, occasionally stealing a rub across my butt or a nibble on my neck.

"Alicia, not that I'm not excited but why did you decide to change your mind? You never let me explain myself."

"Well, I will have to admit raising kids alone is a lot harder than I thought it would be. I want to come home because my babies got to have a cook, janitor, and a chauffeur. Just kidding they need a daddy, and more important I need my big daddy too." I said with a chuckle.

"Oh, that's it. You need your walking, talking, moneymaking vibrator?" Arlington said as he stood behind me grinding on my butt and nibbling on my ear.

"Everything got a purpose. I'm glad you know yours." I said with a smile.

"By the way, the love of your life finally closed the McIntyre account."

"Way to go, see that's my baby. I told you that you could and would do it. You want a chest bump or will a slap on the ass do? Maybe a tongue lashing?"

"Daddy is so creative, that is the only reason I decided to forgive you. I am anxiously anticipating the makeup."

Turning off the lights and heading towards the stairs, I said,

"Oh yeah, I bumped into Piper today and she told me the truth about your relationship with her. She confirmed everything you said. I couldn't hold you responsible because of her lack of judgment." Arlington turned the light back on.

"Alicia, let me make sure I understand. For months you have treated me like change for a nickel, not letting me get two words in edgewise. You accused me of being a liar and took emotional jabs at me every chance you could. Then you bump into the person that started this mess, the person that you have been calling a hoe, slut or whatever degrading name you could find, and believe her over me. Why is what she say, gotta be gospel?"

"It's not like that, bumping into her made me realize how stupid I been acting. Look it shouldn't matter how we got on track, the fact that we are on track is what's important. Let's not forget you were wrong for being involved with her in the first place."

I reached out to Arlington; he pulled away from me, grabbed his keys off the kitchen table and headed to towards the door. I grabbed his arm and he reached for the door handle and said,

"Please don't go, I admit that I was wrong. You mean the world to me and to hear that you were spending time with another woman, literally knocked the wind out of me. I was scared I would lose you. Please don't go I'm begging you."

Arlington turned away from the door and looked at me with disgust; he had such an intense look in his eyes. I was as afraid of what he was about to say, but more afraid of what he would do.

"Alicia my life has been hell for the last six months. I've been a part time father, coming home to an empty house, wrecking my brain, trying to make someone else's wrong right, only for you to turn foot because of someone else. You took Piper's word over mine, now you accept her explanation over mine. What the hell? You know what; I better go before I say something that we both will regret."

Arlington snatched his arm away from me and walked out the door. I could not believe that in a matter of moments I lost my husband all over again. I turned off the kitchen light and headed upstairs to bed. I pulled my dress off, lying on top of the covers in nothing but my black lace panties. I kept replaying the incident in my mind. I laid in silence as I heard the garage close and Arlington drive away. Why did I open my mouth?

"Dad, you up?"

"Yeah Arlington, what's the deal?"

"Man, Alicia called today and basically asked could she come home. I get to the house she was looking good, the kitchen smelling good. I kissed my wife for the first time in six months. Everything was gravy until she told me Piper finally told her that she made up the whole story. How in the hell she keep believing a broad's word over mine? Cassie told her to go so she went. Piper told her come back so she did. When I said I do, I thought I was marrying Alicia not the whole female race. I was so pissed I just left."

"Man, get off my damn phone and take your ass home, make love to your wife and take your ass to sleep. Listen to me son, women got a secret code. They will always listen to each other before they listen to the voice of reason. Your wife is home and that's what you wanted right?"

"Yeah, but."

"But my ass. Go the hell home get you a piece and take your ass to bed."

"Dad, I think I'm so pissed because I have been bending over backwards to mend something I never broke and then just like that I suppose just let everything ride?"

"Son, go home, there is no recourse, and this is what women do. They listen to their emotions and their dumb ass friends. You can try to make her pay, but you will suffer too and at the end of the day, nothing would have changed. She still gonna listen to her friends and you will still be sleeping alone. It doesn't matter how you got it, you got what you wanted. Again, go home."

"Man, I guess you right. I don't know where the hell I thought I was going any damn way. I am in shorts, a t-shirt and slides; I ain't even got my wallet with me."

"Get at me tomorrow."

"Thanks dad."

After about 20 minutes, just as I began to doze off, I heard the garage open. Arlington came back. I was so excited, but I didn't want to get my hopes up just in case he came home only to sleep in the guest room or on the sofa. I heard Arlington come up the stairs. I laid still with my back to the door. He took off his t-shirt, laid behind me and pulled me close to him. Arlington kissed my neck as he squeezed me tightly and whispered,

"I love you."

"I love you too, and I'm sorry. I-"

Arlington interrupted,

"Hush, lay here and go to sleep."

I don't know where Arlington had been, but I closed my eyes and thanked God that he came home and I was finally in my husband's arms again. I peacefully slept as Arlington and I spooned all night long. I finally experienced heaven on earth. I was a little concerned that he didn't want to talk or make love to me.

The next morning, I was awakened by the warmth of the sunlight shining on my face, I was home. I looked over at Arlington just as he was waking up and said,

"Morning."

"Hey you."

I laid on my pillow as Arlington gently rubbed my face with his fingertips, then he leaned in and kissed me on my forehead. I smiled at him.

"Well momma time to get up. You owe me some grits, eggs, steak, and biscuits. Then we gotta get you and the kids moved back in."

"I don't get no loving this morning?"

"Tonight, get up we got things to do."

Arlington quickly jumped out the bed, I can sense his excitement and it felt good. Looking at the glow in his eyes only confirmed that I made the right decision. My life was finally back on track. I sent a text to my girls letting them know what happened but Cassie or Myra never responded. Oh well, they both must be at meetings I thought.

Pawns Have Purpose

I am Cassandra Hughes, better known to my friends as Cassie and I've always been all that! I was born and raised in the bottoms of Florida, but moved to Colorado after my mother inherited some money from some old cousin, aunt or somebody that I didn't know until I went to her funeral. Please don't think I'm insensitive but, I'm glad that she died because that was our ticket out the ghetto. I was not meant to live in poverty. As a little girl, I fantasized about growing up to be a Dallas Cowboy Cheerleader.

I had the moves, body, and definitely the look. I was that girl! I was that girl that stole the attention of every man that crossed my path. I was that girl that all the others girls wanted to be. I was that girl that commanded attention and demanded respect. I didn't believe in taking no prisoners.

No one would have known that I came from the projects. We lived in the good part, if there is such a thing in the hood. I talked proper and dressed nice. I was always the prize to be won. I was the woman that men wanted on their arm, from high school until present day. Yes, your girl always had first pick of the litter. Nobody could lock me down and falling in love damn sure wasn't an option.

If you looked in the encyclopedia for independent, black woman, you found my story. I was too much to be defined by a dictionary. I would describe myself as a hidden treasure not only because I was beautiful, but I was smart as hell.

Book sense and common sense were my forte. I didn't mind hustling so I worked wherever I could get hired until I found that I could make more money and not work as hard in corporate America with my BS. No pun intended. I was able to work a room like nobody's business. I was truly blessed with the gift of gab.

I had been proposed to a million times but, I thought no man was worthy of calling me his own until I met Edmond Chandler. It was a lifetime ago that I dated Edmond, but it seems like it was just yesterday that I fell in love with him. I decided to meet my Auntie Carol for a quick drink before heading home from work.

Auntie Carol was my cool aunt. She was only about 10 years older than me. She never had children of her own or been married, so I was her niece and sista friend. Auntie Carol was knocking on the door of 40, but she still looked like she was every bit of 22. She climbed up the corporate ladder, making her career her life. She was an attorney for many years and recently became a COO of a fortune 100. There was no woman in the world that had accomplished what she had in such a short period of time. Auntie Carol was my mentor and my idol.

Auntie Carol and I sat comparing the woes of our day at work when I noticed a man that stood head and shoulders above the crowd. Without so much as a simple gesture towards me, he had me completely mesmerized. This stranger was someone I just had to meet. His presence commanded authority. I looked at my aunt and said,

"He is going to be my boyfriend. I don't know who he is but I need to meet him." Aunt Carol looked over her shoulder to see who had captured my attention.

"Cassie I don't see nothing back there worth time or attention. Who are you talking about?"

"Auntie, you don't see that tall guy in the NY baseball cap and leather jacket? He needs to be my boyfriend."

Aunt Carol looked over her shoulder again, and then looked back at me as if I was crazy saying,

"Cassie I know damn well you are not talking about that ugly ass man standing against the wall?"

"I care less about what you got to say, that man got swagga and I need to be his boo."

I didn't care what he looked like. I will admit he was a little hard on the eyes, but all I knew was his strong presence was calling me. He stood about 6'6, dark-skinned, with shoulders as wide as a city block. I needed to get a closer gander at him.

"Auntie, I'll be right back, I gotta go get an up close and personal look at my new soon to be boo."

"Leave that man where he's at, that fool looks like the boogie man, king-kong, an over grown gremlin or something. Where you gonna take him? I would be embarrassed to be seen with him in public."

I took a sip of my drink and said,

"I got this, momma be right back."

I made my way across the scarcely crowded club and lingered in front of him for a moment, he didn't even glance in my general direction. I knew I was the most beautiful, best-dressed woman in the club, how dare he not acknowledge me? Since my plan had failed, I decided to keep walking past him to the bathroom. I couldn't look like I was deliberately trying to get his attention.

Besides, I could do a status check in the bathroom to make sure nothing about me was looking out of order. He didn't seem interested, but that didn't stop my desire to meet him. While I was in the bathroom I checked my hair, as usual every strand was in place, the bootie was looking secretly sexy in my suit, and my make-up was flawless. I flashed a flirtatious grin at myself to practice showing it, when I walked past him and back to my table.

I left the bathroom and slowly walked past the stranger again, he still didn't glance at me when I strolled in front of him. He continued talking to his friends like I was invisible.

"I struck out. Auntie, can you believe that he didn't bat an eye when I paraded in front of him twice."

"That's probably a good thing. As ugly as he is, you might have turned to stone."

"Ok, that ain't funny or cute."

"And neither is he so let's keep it moving."

"Whatever, don't hate. I know you are the auntie, but I'mma show you some things."

"Like what? Charity? Just walking past that man is charity, with his ugly ass."

"Don't be mad when I get my prince and you are home alone."

"The good news is I won't be scared of being alone because I know the boogie man will be with you."

Carol and I both chuckled.

"That's a good one. But I'm telling you, I'm seeing something worth having in him. I guess it's time for us to get out of here anyway, besides I gotta go home a devise a plan to meet my new boyfriend."

"Girl, bring your ass and leave your thoughts of that ugly man here."

As I finished my drink, put on my coat and grabbed my purse, I looked up at the stranger again to see if he noticed me. There was still no indication that he even saw me. All the way home, all I could think about was this stranger. Where did he come from? Did he have a girlfriend? How could I get his attention without it looking obvious that I was after him?

Some would argue that I started stalking him. For the next couple weeks, I frequently showed up at the club to watch him. I studied what he drank, I watched who he had around him, and most importantly I watched to see if a female surfaced. The coast was clear. I saw him with the same set of friends and a woman was nowhere to be found.

I drug Auntie Carol to the club with me at least two nights a week to see him. I strategically took a position in the club where I could always be in his line of vision. Once I even bumped into him; without looking at me he said excuse me and kept walking. I could not believe how low I had sunk. I felt like a 16 yr. old trying to get the attention of the captain of the football team. But I was determined to meet this man.

After a month of chasing this fantasy man still not even knowing his name, I thought about giving up. I decided to call my Auntie Carol,

"Ok, I'm giving up. I have tried everything I can think of to meet this man and he still won't even look at me."

"Oh, hell naw. I have listened to you babble about this damn man for over a month. You've drug me to the club night after night just so that you can get a glimpse of him; I am not going to let you walk away that easily. I'll think of something."

"You can try whatever, but I'm convinced he's not interested. Look on the bright side; I'm not dragging you to the club anymore."

I couldn't believe I gave up, but I needed to hold onto some type of dignity. A couple days later, Carol suggested that we go to Axel's. That was a hole in the wall neighborhood club. I was surprised when my fantasy man walked over to our table, extended his hand to me and said,

"I'm Edmond and you are?"

I couldn't help but flash a flirtatious grin as I shook his hand.

"My name is Cassie, and it's great to meet you."

"Well Cassie, it's a pleasure to meet you. It's nice to see you again Carol. I'll send the waitress over so I can buy ya'll a drink. You ladies have a good evening."

Just as quick as Edmond appeared, he abruptly disappeared. I was real confused. Carol noticed the puzzled look on my face.

"Ok, let me come clean. After we talked the other night, I decided to take matters into my own hands. I came here by myself. I introduced myself to him and told him that I had a niece that was interested in meeting him. He is quite a gentleman; he bought me a drink and asked me questions about you like, your name and why you wanted to meet him. I told him that you had seen him around and thought he was good looking. Without hesitation he said ok, and asked if I would bring you here tonight."

"I can't believe you put me out there like that but thank you. I just don't understand why he's not interested. You see he shook my hand, bought me a drink and exited stage left immediately."

"I think he is interested; he's just not used to women approaching him. Don't trip."

A million thoughts raced through my mind as I sipped my drink and talked to Carol. Now that I had a drink in my system or shall I say a little liquid courage, I decided to approach him. I walked up to Edmond and asked,

"So when are you gonna take me on a date?"

He chuckled and said,

"You want to go on a date with me?"

"Yes, I want to get to know you better."

"Wow, ok I guess."

Edmond turned to the bar and wrote his cellular number, his business number and his home number on a napkin. I looked at the napkin.

"Ok, which number is the best contact number for you? I don't want to feel like I'm stalking you or anything."

"My cell."

"I will call you tomorrow; don't act like you don't know who I am when I call."

"I promise I won't ever forget you. But you don't have to wait until tomorrow, you can call me tonight."

Edmond responded with a huge grin on his face. I smiled back at him as I walked away. I finally had the number of the man of my dreams, and we were going on our first date. I was as giddy as a goofy goose. I sat back at the table with Carol still on cloud nine.

"Ok, girl you are grinning so hard that you are blinding me. I assume things went well?"

"Yes. He asked me to call me tonight and we are going on a date tomorrow."

"See after all that, look how easy that was. But no you had to stalk the poor man for a month."

After leaving the club, I got comfortable at home and gave Edmond a call. We had very general conversation. You know the sky is blue, water is wet, do you think Broncos are going to win the game on Sunday type of conversation. He did marvel at the fact that I wanted to meet him because he thought I was so beautiful. I told him how attractive I thought he was and I was honored that he gave me his number.

The moment of truth was finally here, Edmond and I decided to meet for dinner after I got off work. I lived in the suburbs, and he lived in the inner city so he decided to come on my side of town.

We met at a steakhouse for dinner. We sat at the table talking and getting acquainted. That was when I found out that Edmond was 42 and I was 25. The age difference didn't seem to matter to either one of us. I noticed during our conversation, all he was doing was smiling and staring at me. I finally asked,

"Why are you staring at me?"

"You are just gorgeous, absolutely gorgeous. I can't understand why you wanted to meet me."

"I was at Axel's one night and you stole my attention. You are just so attractive to me."

"Oh no not me, I can't get over how gorgeous you are." I smiled and said thank you.

"That's what I am going to call you from now on. Your name is Gorgeous." I smiled.

After dinner he insisted that I ride with him to his business. I would have never guessed that he was a business owner, but he owned an arcade. When we walked in through the back entrance, we were met by his brother and a few of his friends. Edmond introduced me to everyone as Gorgeous.

After meeting everyone, I sat quietly on a stool. Raymond, a guy that I dated in high school walked in. When I spoke to Raymond, he casually responded. I wasn't sure he recognized me because it had been more than 7 years since we saw each other.

Edmond and Raymond engaged in a personal conversation out of my earshot. I assumed it was something that I didn't need or want to know. Raymond pulled out an electronic phone book as they talked. I entertained myself in the meantime with a game of Tetris. After about 15 minutes Raymond walked out the door and Edmond escorted me to his office in the back of the arcade.

"I need to tell you a few things about me."

I took a deep breath. I just knew Edmond was about to tell me that he was married, gay, had six baby mommas or something. I know it was just our first date but I was already attached to him. With hesitation I responded,

"What do you need to tell me?"

"I'm on parole. A few years ago I got caught trying to buy 4 kilos from the feds. I did 4 years behind bars and I got 4 years on paper. The good news is, I only got one year left. That is why I own my own business. Being a felon there aren't many job opportunities for me. Truthfully, I've never done anything but deal."

I really didn't know what to say. I didn't care about where he had been. I was just excited that he found his way to me. From what I could tell, he was living a straight and narrow life now and that's all that mattered to me.

"We all have a past, but I appreciate you trusting me enough to share that with me."

"Gorgeous and sweet, I still don't understand what you see in me?" Edmond said as he hugged me tightly.

From that moment our love affair began to flourish. Edmond and I were inseparable. My life became a modern day beauty and the beast fairytale. We laughed, ate and spent time simply getting to know each other. Edmond lived in the hood and was educated on the streets yet, he treated me as if I was a precious jewel. Edmond wasn't very polished, professional, or knew anything other than the streets. But, I fell in love with him, before I realized it. There was nothing he wouldn't do for me.

Edmond catered to my every need. When I was with him I felt safe, secure, and most of all adored. No one or nothing else mattered when we were together. Edmond treated me like a man is supposed to treat a woman. He was respectful of me and my house. I remember one night we met for a drink in separate cars, he sent his friend out to dust the snow off my car and warm it up for me. When we were out together people often commented on how much in love we looked. I was so glad Carol took matters into her own hands and initiated things between Edmond and I. This was the first time I had ever been in love.

My favorite pass time was eating. I showed him the world outside the hood. I took him to places that were common to me but he had never heard of. We would look into one another eyes and simply smile, and at least once a day he would say,

"Gorgeous you are so gorgeous why do you want someone like me?"

"You are absolutely wonderful and I couldn't ask for anyone better. I consider myself the lucky one."

I spent all my free time with Edmond. Myra, Alicia, and Auntie Carol thought I had vanished from the face of the earth because I hadn't seen them in months. We decided to meet for happy hour. When I made it to the bar, Aunt Carol and the girls were already sitting with their drinks.

"Now how are ya'll gonna start without me?"

"Edmond has had you on lock for so long that I thought you forgot how to be by yourself."

Alicia said as she held her hand up for some dap.

"Ok, he is on your arm so much I thought he was an accessory." Myra said as she slapped Alicia a high five.

"Myra, look at you co-signing. Drink your juice and leave me alone with ya'll hatin' asses."

It seems like it has been forever since we all have been together, but I was glad to be with my girls.

"Girl you are just glowing. Edmond must be hitting all the corners."

"Shut up Alicia it ain't even like that. Although a sista been getting it twice a day damn near every day."

"I'm just trying to figure out why we ain't met the mystery man yet? Does he really exist? I ain't never seen you keep something a secret this long."

"Yes he does exist, we've just been spending time together really getting to know one another. At any rate, what's been going on?"

Me and the girls sat for over an hour playing catch up. I really missed my girls. Out the corner of my eye, I saw Edmond walk in. He didn't know where I was meeting the girls so this was a pleasant surprise. The girls noticed immediately that I had tuned them out with the overwhelming smile that radiated from me.

"You know who must have just walked in the door. Look who is all lit up like Broadway?"

Auntie Carol said as she shook her head.

"Stop it ain't even that serious. But look at that man! He is head and shoulders above the crowd. You see that he gets mad respect."

"What in the ham n cheese are you talking about Cassie? I know you are not talking about that tall, ugly guy in the baseball cap that is heading this way." Myra said with a crazy expression on her face.

"Yep, that's him. I told her that he wasn't no kind of catch. But she insisted on dating him. But beauty is in the eye of the beholder."

"With all due respect Auntie Carol, there ain't nothing beholding that. Cassie you can't be for real?" Alicia said as she glanced back and forth at Edmond as he walked to the table.

"At least we know why we ain't seen you in a month of Sundays, that booga bear has had you hibernating with him."

"Get it together ladies. Here he comes." I said as I stood up from my chair to hug Edmond as he approached. I introduced him to everyone. The ladies were cordial and polite as he shook their hands and hugged Auntie Carol.

"Ladies it was a pleasure finally meeting you and it was great seeing you again Carol. But I'm gonna get out of here so ya'll can do ya'll girl stuff. Honey, I'll see you at home tonight." Edmond said as he kissed me on the lips good bye.

"I just love that man."

"Hell somebody got to. Girl, if you like it I love it, do you?" Alicia said as she shook her head. Just a few seconds later, the waitress returned to the table.

"Here's a round for everyone, compliments of that gentleman over there."

"Ok, that was a power move right there. We might have to keep your field hand of a man."

"Whatever Alicia, I love him and I will be spending the rest of my life with him."

"Let me quit talking about your man."

I was so engaged with the girls that I didn't even notice when Edmond snuck out. I can't believe that he didn't say good bye. Edmond and I had been dating for about six months before he made a move to have sex with me. I was lucky to get a hug and an open mouth kiss from him. He was always a complete gentleman.

My birthday had finally rolled around. Edmond asked me what I wanted him to buy me. I know men don't like to shop and Edmond was not going to spend too much time outside his hood. I decided to write him a list of 5 items and let him choose the one he wanted me to have. I was surprised when he showed up at my birthday party with five gifts.

The most exciting gift on my birthday was Edmond dressed up for me. He always wore jeans and tennis shoes no matter what. The fact that he put on a suit for me almost made me cry because he never wore his Sunday best, unless he was going to a funeral.

I had met most of Edmond's family and he supported me in everything I did. I think finally we were moving our relationship to that next level. You guessed it, we were finally gonna get our swerve on.

I was looking forward to making love to Edmond for the first time. His touch was sensual yet delicate. I could tell that Edmond was nervous about making love to me because he continuously hesitated as he removed my clothes and touched my most secret places. I knew in my mind that this was a special moment for both of us. Edmond securely held me as we made love. Thoughts of Edmond were the only thing that filled my mind. This man was my world.

After Edmond and I made love he held me in his arms.

"Gorgeous are you ok?"

"Yes, I am. Are you ok?"

"Yeah, I just wanted to make sure that I didn't hurt you or make you do anything that you didn't want to do."

"Edmond I love you and I know that you love me. I also know that you would never do anything to hurt me. Look at this smile, you did this. I never knew that I could be happy every day until I met you."

Edmond kissed me on the forehead,

"Gorgeous you are so sweet. I don't deserve you."

"I believe that you do. You are the best and you deserve the best and that's me."

Edmond just chuckled as he ran his fingers through my hair. I kissed a frog and got a prince, boy was I lucky. For the next several months, Edmond and I continued to see each other almost daily. He spent the night over my house almost every night. I guess some would say that we were living together. He had a few essentials at my house and when he turned his mobile phone off people called my house phone looking for him. He was a reason worth living.

I began to know more and more about Edmond's life or shall I say his past. He finally reached the last of his probation and was going to be off paper for good. I was ready to celebrate. Me and daddy were gonna go to the Bahamas, Jamaica, Mexico, or wherever there was going to be peace and sun.

Edmond began to introduce me to more and more of his family, but I had not met his daughter Kelly yet. Kelly was 16 and her mother died when Kelly was 5 and Edmond had custody of her ever since. I knew when I met her; it would be time to pull out the wedding bells. He talked about how he loved kids and girls were his favorite. Ok I could definitely give him a chocolate baby girl that looked just like her momma. I loved him and all but it would be a disaster if my daughter looked like him.

It had been a year since Edmond, and I became official. I thought I was the luckiest girl in the world. One night I followed Edmond from the club to his job. We sat in his truck and talked before it was time for him to start his shift. We began to talk about life and love when Edmond said,

"I once loved a woman so much that I gave her kids my name."

All I could say to myself was wow! This is the very reason that I was going to marry this man very soon. I kissed Edmond goodbye and left his job. I was about halfway home when it dawned on me that Edmond just said, he loved a woman enough that he gave her kids his name. That meant the woman had to have had his name also. I made a wide U-turn in the middle of the street. I needed to know where this woman and her kids were. Up to this point he never mentioned a wife, or kids other than Kelly.

When I made it back to his job, I asked him to come out and talk to me.

"Baby, are you ok. What's wrong Gorgeous?" He asked as he approached my car.

"You're married aren't you?"

"Who told you that?"

"Just answer the question. Are you married?"

"Yes, I have been married for 14 years now."

I wasn't gonna let him see me cry. I got in my car and pulled off without muttering a sound and releasing the first tear. A couple of blocks away I had to pull over. I was crying so hard that I could not see. I have never in my life felt such betrayal, not just because Edmond was married but because no one in his family ever told me either. I can only imagine that they thought of me as a home wrecking whore.

I heard the faint sound of my mobile phone ringing. I pulled it out of my jacket pocket to see that it was Edmond. I couldn't talk to him because he would know that I was crying, so I turned the phone off. I finally made it home and cried myself to sleep.

The next morning my eyes were so swollen from crying that I could barely open them. I placed a cold towel on my eyes so the swelling would go down enough for me to go to work. I never bothered turning on my phone as I got dressed for work. I have never been so humiliated in my life. I headed out the door. Lord knows I didn't want to deal with my crazy ass co-workers today.

They were liable to get the psychotic Cassie today. Much to my surprise, Edmond was standing at my car with a bushel of roses. I was interested in where he found such beautiful roses at 7 o'clock in the morning.

"Oh what you picked those out of your wife's garden before you came over here?"

"No I bought them for you, I'm sorry."

"I can't talk about this right now, I gotta go to work."

"Can I come over after work so we can talk?"

"What is there to talk about? How you made me look like a fool? Or, wait you can always feed me that married man we're not together lie."

"Ok, I wasn't honest with you but, let me tell you what's going on. You know I have a key to your place, so I don't need permission to come by, I'm just being courteous by asking you nicely."

"That's fine whatever, I gotta go to work, take the flowers in the house. I'll see you after work."

I couldn't focus at all that day. I couldn't believe Edmond. I could not believe I got played like this. I made it through the day on a hope and a prayer. I went straight home after work. Edmond was there just like he said he would be.

"Hey."

"How was your day?"

"It was as good as it could be, considering the foul way that it got started."

"Before you start cooking, come sit down so I can tell you what's up."

"Please do because I need to know why you got all this extra going on?"

I sat on the couch and just looked at Edmond like he was change for a nickel. He rubbed his hands together, and then sat in the chair on the other side of the coffee table.

"Gorgeous like I said last night, I married Michelle that's my wife's name. Fourteen years ago, I met her soon after Kelly's mother died. When I got into all that trouble she stayed right there, she had my back and I do love her."

"Where she at?"

"What do you mean? She's at home I guess."

"So you aren't separated, getting a divorce or anything?"

"I can't lie to you, I can't leave her. She wanted me when no one else did and she stayed with me when I went to jail and everything. She is the only momma Kelly has ever really known."

"Well, I'm not in search of a wife in law so I'm good. So your wife just let you stay out all night?"

"No she works nights. She's a nurse. Gorgeous I love you and I never meant to hurt you. We got something special and I'm not trying to lose you."

"The last time I checked, there is nothing special about being the side boo. See I'm not like the hood rats that you are used to dealing with. I don't need you. You are in my life because I chose you. I allow you to be with me."

"I never thought a woman like you would want to be with me, I didn't take you seriously when you said that you wanted to go out with me. That is why I didn't tell you about my wife, I never thought things between us were gonna go anywhere."

I thought I was a fairly intelligent woman, but I was really confused. Edmond just told me that he loves me but he isn't going to leave his wife.

"I need to understand how you could say that you love me, but you can only give me a part of you. I will never be a priority in your life. I would never have holidays and if my car left me stranded on the side of the road, chances are, you would not be able to come and get me. Baby that ain't love!"

"Gorgeous, if you were stranded on the side of the road and I couldn't get to you, you better believe that I would make damn sure I would send somebody to handle it for me. Believe that."

Edmond missed the point of what I was trying to say. I couldn't think, my head was pounding, and I didn't have the energy or desire to keep going with this conversation.

"Edmond I need you to leave. I had a long day at work and I can't deal with this right now. Please do that for me and I promise that I will call you tomorrow so we can talk."

"I will respect that. Can I call and check on your later?"

"No, I will call you tomorrow."

I walked Edmond to the door; he leaned in to kiss me on the lips. I turned away so that his peck landed on my cheek.

"You promise to call me tomorrow?"

"Yes, I promise. Good night."

I was so glad that he was gone. How did a perfect dream become a nightmare with the simple utterance of a single sentence? I needed some advice. I prayed that Alicia would be available for dinner. I called Alicia and we made plans to meet in an hour. Thank God she was available. I had just enough time to change clothes and meet her. Alicia and I met at Senor Miguel's. Whenever we go to Miguel's that means we have to discuss. The timing was impeccable; we pulled up at the same time. Alicia, got out the car and shouted,

"Hey lady. Are the other divas late today?"

"I was not in the mood for a roll call. I need someone on one attention today."

"What's up girl? Do we need to get a drink first?"

"Let's go inside and we will holla at you?"

I walked behind Alicia as the hostess took us to a booth. We immediately dug into the chips and salsa. I began to spill my guts before the waiter came to take our order.

"Why is Edmond married?"

"Edmond, married to who? I thought you was the only one that would give him the time of day."

Usually I play along and defend Edmond when my girls start dogging me about Edmond not being the cutest doll on the shelf, but this time, I didn't even crack a smile.

"You must be serious. How did you find out?"

"Well, last night we went out for a quick drink before he went to work, we were talking and he said that he loved a woman so much that he gave her kids his last name. It took me a minute to put two and two together but now you have it. I got a whole wife in law."

"Shut up, what are you gonna go?"

"Hell if I know. That is why I'm here with you."

"I'm sorry but how is his ugly ass trying to play somebody? Haven't you been to his house, met his family and stuff?"

"Well, it turns out the house I went to is his brother's house. It has always been more convenient for him to spend the night at my house. And, I'm mad I have met his other brother's wife several times and she never said a word."

"I know blood is supposed to be thicker than water, but I will be damned if my husband's brother brings his side boo around me because I would think that my husband was doing the same thing when I wasn't around."

"Cassie that fool is at your house more than you are. Where does his wife be?"

"This brotha earned the pimp of the year award. She works nights and I workdays so he ain't got to lie to nobody about nothing. Time management is a bitch ain't it?"

I laid all the cards on the table for Alicia. Then asked so what should I do?"

"Cassie you my girl and I got your back. Listen, if I was you I would keep him. You know what you're dealing with; deal with it on that level. He don't demand nothing from you, he worships the ground you walk on, and gives you everything that you can imagine. Ride it out. You can do what you wanna do, but I'm just saying you get all the benefits with none of the work."

I cannot believe that my best friend is encouraging me to become a home wrecker.

"For real Alicia, you think it is ok for me to sleep with a married man?"

"Well you have been sleeping with him for what 6 months now? Apparently they have an understanding of some sort. Edmond is gone more than he is at home. I wouldn't be surprised if she had a side thing too. I'm pretty sure she knows he's cheating but there is a reason that she ain't left him yet. No I don't condone cheating but you have nothing to lose and everything to gain. Tell the truth, you don't want to get married right now; you just want to marry him. Am I wrong?"

"You do make a good point?"

"Look at it this way, what has or will change now that you know he's married? Is he gonna cut back his hours with you, quit spending money, what? You are at a better advantage now. Get all that you need and want out the relationship and when he's tired of playing house with you, he will take his blocks and go home. And you ain't lost nothing."

"That is the truth all day long. You are right; most women would kill to have a man like Edmond without any obligation."

I felt better about the situation. He dealt the cards; all I can do is play the hand that he gave me. I thought I knew in my heart what I wanted to do all along; I just needed to bounce it off someone.

"Well enough about me and my problems. What's going on in your life?"

"Not a damn thing. Single and hatin every minute of it."

"You are married to your career; you ain't got no room in your life for a man right now."

"Yeah, you're right but it sounded good.
Let's get outta here. I think you got this under control."

"Alright girl, let's get out of here. I'll holla at you after I talk to him."

"Are you gonna tell him what's up tonight? Naw, I think he should stew for a while. I'm going to call him after I leave the office tomorrow."

"Let, him sweat, but don't give him none for a few days. Let him miss it."

"Bye girl."

As I drove home, I was excited. As far as I'm concerned, me, Edmond, and his wife was getting what we wanted. When I got back home, I was able to relax and go to bed with no concerns. It seemed like the clock in the office was only moving a second every half hour or so. I was trying to read a few of my upcoming cases, but I could not get my mind off of Edmond and the phone call I was going to make after work. I kept picking up the phone to dial his number, but I caught myself before reaching the seventh digit.

At lunchtime, I reached into my purse for my makeup bag when I noticed that I had several missed calls from Edmond. I had him right where I wanted him. I resisted the urge to call him back. I was not going to let him think he had me caught up.

After what seemed to be an eternity, 5 o'clock finally came. As soon as I got in my car, I called Edmond and invited him over. About 20 minutes later, I got home to see his car in my driveway. How did he beat me home? Damn was he sitting at my house all day? As soon as I walked in the door, Edmond started apologizing to me and telling me how much he loved me.

"Edmond, we got to talk about this."
I led Edmond to the couch so that we could sit down.

"Baby, what do you want to talk about? I'll do whatever, as long as you promise not to leave me."

"No, I'm not going to leave you. I love you and you are the best man that I ever had. You will love me enough to make me your wife."

Edmond got on his knees, laid his head on my stomach and held me tightly.

"Thank you Gorgeous, thank you."

For the rest of the evening, Edmond and I cuddled on the couch. Life was perfect. I thank God I didn't let my emotions get the best of me.

After a few days of hesitation on my part and plenty of making up on Edmond's part, we were in love and back on track. It seemed as though things between Edmond and I was moving in a positive progression for us. I was walking on sunshine beneath the stars. At that moment I felt sorry for anyone that hadn't experienced love like this before.

I was supposed to meet Edmond for happy hour the night before I was headed out of town for a business trip. Edmond didn't show up. When I called him, his phone rang directly to voice mail. I was a little concerned but no big deal, there were things that I needed to do. I knew he was busy; he would never intentionally stand me up. The next morning, I headed out of town as if nothing was wrong.

I flew to Chicago for a conference. I love Chicago. I could see the lakefront from my hotel. It was majestic, perfect for a beach side stroll with the man of my dreams. I called Edmond, he didn't answer his phone. Now I was a little concerned, it has been damn near two days and I hadn't talked to him. I wasn't liking this at all.

Edmond called me the following morning. I was in the conference and missed his call by seconds. When I tried to call back, he didn't answer. What in the hell was really going on. Edmond and I played phone tag for the rest of the day. I called before I boarded my plane, and he finally answered.

"Edmond, what's up is everything all right?"

"Yeah I'm good. Why?"

"Well, I haven't talked to you in a couple days."

"That doesn't mean that something is wrong. You are supposed to be out of town taking care of business not thinking about me."

"I always think about you and still handle my business. I'm coming home today. I land about 6 o'clock will you be there when I get home?"

"Yes, I can swing by."

"Ok, they are boarding the plane. See you tonight, I love you."

"Alright."

Edmond hung up the phone without telling me that he loved me. That was weird. I wonder who he was with.

I landed back in Denver and went straight home, much to my surprise Edmond wasn't there. I unpacked, got comfortable and laid across the bed.

Before I knew it, it was morning. Edmond never showed up. I checked my phones, no missed calls and nothing in the caller id. I didn't know what to think. Me and Edmond was happy and in love, what changed in just a couple of days?

After I got dressed for work, I called Edmond, no answer. I went into the office and got caught up on my cases and all my other pending work. No word from Edmond. He called me at home when he knew I was at work and vice versa. I called him from another desk at the office and he picked up the phone.

"Edmond, what's up? I've been trying to reach you. What happened to you last night?"

"I was just about to call you Gorgeous. How is your day going?"

"It good, but you didn't answer my question. Why did you leave me hanging last night?"

"Let's meet for dinner at 6 over at Jasmine's. I'm in the mood for a good steak. Cool?"

"Yeah, that's fine. I'll see you then."

I agreed to meet him for dinner. I was missing him like crazy; I guess we'll talk about what's going on at dinner. Every time I did manage to get Edmond on the phone to ask him a question, we acted like he didn't hear me or like he didn't care what I was feeling. It was time for me to confront him and get some answers. I wrapped things up at office I headed to Jasmine's. I waited and called for over 30 minutes.

Edmond was a no call, no show. I had it, I decided to go find him and make him face me like a man and tell me what was wrong with us. We went from puppy dogs, tulips, and rainbows, to hell and high water in 24 hours. Somebody needed to tell me something.

I drove by his brother's house, all his favorite hang outs, and Edmond was nowhere to be found. I tried calling no answer. What in the hell was wrong with me? Was I really stalking an ugly, married man? I gathered myself and took my happy hips home. Two days had passed and I had not heard from Edmond. I didn't bother dialing his digits either, but I consistently thought about him.

After a week had passed and I had not received a return call, I knew I had to do something. I couldn't control myself. It was time for me to make him talk to me. I knew exactly where and what time I could find him. I showed up at his job. I was waiting in the parking lot when he pulled up. I got out of the car and confronted him.

"Hey remember me? I'm supposed to be the love of your life."

"What are you doing here?"

"Well, you won't call, you keep standing me up. What else am I supposed to do?"

"Let me go clock in and then I'll be back out here. Go sit in my truck, I'll be right back."

I took the keys out of his hands and headed to his truck. About 10 minutes later, I see Edmond walking out of the warehouse. I waited until he got into the truck. I didn't say anything, I just looked at him.

"What do you want to talk about? It's late and you gotta go to work in the morning."

"I need to know what's going on with us."

"There's nothing going on?"

"Let's try this again, why are you being so shady towards me? One day you tell me you love me, then I can't get you to talk to me, see me or anything. Tell me what's really going on."

"It's late, you shouldn't even be here you got work in the morning. Go home and I will call you tomorrow."

"No you will not pimp me off again. Tell me what in the hell is going on?" I said as loud and matter fact as I could.

"Look at you. You're getting upset, just calm down and I'll tell you."

"You better tell me something or we will be out here all damn night."

Edmond fumbled around in the truck. Then he took his baseball cap off, scratched his head before he put the cap back on, all in silence.

"I'm listening, what's so hard for you to talk about, tell me what you got to say." Edmond hesitated for a minute, then he took a deep breath and finally began to talk to me.

"Gorgeous, remember when we first met and Raymond came into the arcade to holla at me?"

"Yeah, that was a year or so ago? What does that have to do with anything?"

"Well, I asked him what was up with ya'll. Well, he pulled out his personal organizer and started showing me men that you used to talk to."

I had no idea where this conversation was going, but I wished he would quit stumbling over his words and get to the point. I let him continue before I interrupted.

"Later that night while we were gambling at the gambling shack and your name came up. Raymond, Jack, and some of the other fellas was all there clowning me. They were saying that you were outta of my league. I really didn't stand a chance with you. That you would never love me and that you were only with me because of the money. The bet was on the table that I couldn't make you my woman and that you would never give me some ass."

I kept listening,

"You know me as a betting man, so I took the bet. Inside I knew that they were right. I thought you were just playing around when you said you wanted to go out with me. I wasn't gonna let them just punk me like that. I never thought you really liked me or would grow to love me, and I definitely never thought I would love you. I was never supposed to love you."

"You know what's funny, Ray, Jack and a couple other brothas that you know tried to holla at me over the years. Even with their Benzes and whatever, I never gave any of them the time of day. They were just hatin' on you and you were too stupid to notice. Edmond, I don't understand, why in the fuck didn't you let me go months ago when I found out that you were married?"

I didn't give Edmond a chance to answer the question. I turned away from Edmond. I felt like someone had gut punched me and then stabbed me in the heart. I couldn't look at him. I held my head down as tears rolled down my face. I got out of his truck and headed to my car without saying a word or looking back. It took everything in my soul to keep my composure until I walked into my house. I felt like my heart was being torn from my body. I never knew heartache was for real and physical.

When I got in my house I could barely breathe because my heart hurt so bad. My cell phone rang a few times, but I couldn't pick up the phone. The pain in my heart had me paralyzed. I got in bed fully dressed trying to find the tears in hopes that it would relieve the pain. I was hurt so bad that all I could do was rock myself to sleep. I took Alicia's advice to keep seeing him, but never told my heart to stop loving him.

For days my eyes were dry and my heart ached. All I could do is come home from work, get in the bed until it was time for me to go to work the next morning. I looked a mess; I refused to wear makeup or jewelry. Thank God, I was still just a law clerk and didn't have to face anybody. I felt like a part of me was gone.

After hiding out for a week, I called the girls and told them that Edmond broke up with me, but I never told them why. I was too embarrassed to admit that I was played like a fiddle. Then I called Auntie Carol to tell her what happened. She tried to comfort me by saying,

"He didn't deserve you and he wasn't even cute anyway don't trip."

I understand that Auntie Carol was trying to cheer me up and make me look on the bright side, nevertheless I loved him.

This was the first time I had ever been in love more importantly this was the first time I had been rejected. I had no idea what I was supposed to be feeling, or what to do to make it go away. I began to function as best as I could.

One day Auntie Carol decided to come check on me, only to find me in bed, with the blind shut, and the television on some informational. I'm glad she had a key, because I wasn't getting up for no one short of Jesus Himself.

"Oh my, you are really hurting. I didn't believe it until now, but you really did love that man?"

All I could do is give her a close-lipped smile and nod yes. That was when the floodgates opened. I cried like I have never cried in my life.

"Oh God why? Why God?" I screamed as I rocked back and forth holding myself. Carol started to cry and held me as I rocked.

"Why did he do this to me? All I did was love him."

"I'm so sorry Cassie, I wish I could take the pain away."

I continued to cry uncontrollably until I just fell asleep. I don't know when Carol left. I just woke up the next morning with a headache.

For months, I went on with my life trying desperately to forget that Edmond ever existed, but everything reminded me of him. I became a recluse.

I spent my time growing plants. Before I realized it I had more than 28 plants covering my two-bedroom town home. I got my hair braided and stopped wearing makeup. I refused to date, I guess I slipped into depression.

Occasionally, I would see Edmond, we casually acknowledged each other never talking about what happened between us but things remained tense. It's funny how I lived in Denver almost all my life and never met Edmond, now that he had broken my heart, I see his ass regularly. One afternoon I went to pick my car up from the mechanic, Edmond was there.

"Hey Gorgeous, I already paid for the repairs on your car."

"Thank you. How much do I owe you?"

"You owe me dinner. Let me buy you dinner tonight and we'll call it even."

"Ok, let's meet around the corner at Friday's."

"That's good. I'll follow you there."

I had no idea what to expect from dinner or why I received the invitation. I went into the restaurant ahead of Edmond, I didn't want it to feel like a date. I hoped he didn't ask me here to tear the scab off my wound. It had been a year since we broke up, yet tension still existed. Dinner was awkward; I could barely bring myself to look at him. We ate in silence. Finally, Edmond decided to break the ice.

"Gorgeous you know what, I miss you. I miss dinners like these. You know you took me to places that I have never been before. I'm sorry that I hurt you and things ended the way they did. You are a wonderful, beautiful woman that has so much to offer and deserve so much more than I could have ever offered you. Even if I left my wife, you deserve better than me. I am not saying what I did was right."

I could not believe what I was hearing; I just stared at him as he kept talking.

"I never intended to tell you about the bet. I tried to do things to make you quit me, but you stayed by my side and that made me love you even more. I could never survive in your world. You deserve to be more than street bootie and you damn sure deserve someone better than me. I love you enough to see you happy. You are so strong and I knew what I was doing would hurt you, but I also knew that you would survive. I chose to let you hurt for a little while than to see you hurt for a lifetime. Think of it this way, I snatched the bandage off fast."

I smiled and remembered why I fell in love with him in the beginning. At that moment I felt like I was set free. I had the closure that I needed to open a door to opportunities. We sat smiling at each other and said good-bye. What we had will always be special to me and as time passes and we see each other, he still calls me Gorgeous with a smile, and I thank God for him.

It was that defining moment that became the catalyst of me snapping back. I made a vow to myself that I would never allow another man to hurt me like that again. I promised myself that I would never shed a tear over a man again. As soon as I got home, I took those braids out my head, relaxed my hair, looked in the mirror and smiled at myself. I clutched my strength and power with both hands never to give it away again.

I don't know what it was about that dinner. I felt empowered and ready to go around the world once and see everybody twice. I had been putting off the bar examine forever. The lawyers at the firm were riding me about getting that done. The next day I registered for the bar and began to transform from being a lady and take my rightful place as a woman! Look out world here I come. Just call me Hellava.

The Bishop's Queen

I think I was about six years old when my family moved into the suburbs of Denver. I think Denver was the fourth city in six years that my family had lived in. My father was in the Air Force and had traveled the world before I was born. I think we ended up in Denver because my mother refused to move again. I am Myra Patrice Asbury, my parent's only child and my father's pride and joy.

There seemed to be no children in my neighborhood, I think everybody had dogs instead of children. I know at six years old, I didn't know a lot, but I knew I didn't like Denver. I guess somebody at the base, a neighbor, or somebody recommended a church for us to join. I remember that day because my mother gave me one side ponytail and left the back hanging in banana curls.

I felt like a big girl walking into Sunday school wearing a pastel print dress, white patent leather shoes with the matching purse filled with my Barbie's accessories. Because I felt so cute, I didn't care that I didn't know any of the other kids in the room. My mother asked if I was ok, I nodded yes to reassure her that I would be ok being left alone and that I would not cry.

I was escorted by the Sunday school teacher to an empty chair close to her. As soon as my butt touched the chair, I felt my butt hit the floor. The boy next to me pulled the chair from underneath me. It amazes me I don't remember my

Sunday school teacher's name, but I remember her telling me that Braxton Clemons, the Pastor's son only pushed me down because he liked me. I didn't cry when I saw that Braxton made me snag my tights on something. The battle with Braxton didn't end there, during our Bible story time; he pulled my hair and blamed it on the boy sitting next to him.

I would not have ever guessed that not only would I be introduced to the Lord as my personal savior, but also be introduced to my future husband. Church was the foundation of me and Braxton's relationship, before either one of us was allowed to date; we got to see each other at least twice a week at church.

As the years passed Braxton and I got older we became inseparable. He knew how to play the keyboard and I sang in the choir. It seemed like he played to the tune of my beating heart. As his talent grew so did my love for him. Before it was ever official, everyone at church said that they thought we made the cutest, most ideal couple.

Not only was Braxton being shaped into a perfect man of God and groomed to eventually receive the mantle from his father and lead the church, but he was also a star basketball player. We went to different high schools, but it wasn't too hard to keep up with him. He seemed to make the front page of the sports page every week since his freshman year.

When Braxton became a starter on the varsity team, the coaches, sport enthusiasts, and even Braxton himself knew he was destined for a career in the NBA, but God had different plan for him. Braxton would be ordained and was going to take his rightful place in the church and be elevated to the office of Bishop. And, I was going to be by his side as his first lady cheering him on every step of the way.

Watching Braxton was like watching two people operate simultaneously. He was that star to everyone else, but

I saw the man, the essence of who he really was. I remember the first time he taught Bible study in his father's absence. The anointing was on Braxton and the Spirit moved as he ministered to us about Shadows. He preached Psalm 23 like he wrote that chapter himself. I hung on his every word and inserted my "Amens" in the right places. I found myself just staring at him in admiration.

I was overwhelmed by what I was witnessing. The pulpit was where Braxton was God's point guard. After service one of the church mothers came to me and said,

"God told me to tell you that He has heard your prayers. Minister Braxton is your husband, continue to wait on the Lord and He will give you the desires of your heart."

"Thank you, Mother, I receive that in the name of Jesus." I knew she was speaking a word straight from the Lord because it was confirmation to what I already knew. I was destined to become Mrs. Braxton Clemons. Girls chased Braxton, bought him stuff, but he never gave them the time of day. Braxton never said we were a couple, but everyone at church knew it, so they called me his girlfriend. Actually, I was the closest thing to a girlfriend that he had.

Spring 1995, I was a junior in high school. My prayers began to manifest themselves. Braxton asked me to escort him to his senior prom. This was going to be our first public appearance to the world. Braxton was a year older than I was. He was on a college recruiting visit last year so he missed his junior prom. But at last, I was going to be showcased in front of all the hood rats, groupies, and gold diggers. They were finally about to see why they didn't get no love from Braxton.

The evening was magical. Braxton showed up at my house in a black stretch limousine. He sat in the family room talking with my father as I remained upstairs with my mother adorning me with the finishing touches. My mother finally said that I looked good enough to present myself to Braxton. I stood at the top of the stairs, in my diamond studs that I got for my sixteenth birthday and a Tiffany's blue strapless, tea length dress. Every strand my hair was molded into a perfect French roll.

At first sight both my father and Braxton stood up. Braxton's face exuded his excitement. While pride shined on my father's face. As I began my processional down the staircase, my father looked at Braxton and said,

"That is my little girl. I spoiled her for a reason. If you can't take care of her, then you need to leave her at home."

"With all due respect, I got this. I will handle your porcelain doll as a precious jewel. I'm just honored to be in the company of such grace and beauty."

All I could do was smile. I was on cloud nine. When we walked into the prom, I would swear I watched the room part to receive us as if we were royalty entering a great ball. Braxton made me feel welcome and comfortable although I didn't know anyone in the room. I felt special because he introduced me to everyone by name and as his girl. This was only the prelude to the social engagements and special events that we were destined to share throughout our relationship together.

In the middle of July, I went to the Clemons house as they packed Braxton up for college. As an athlete, they were required to check into the dorms several weeks before the other students. I had to make sure that I sent him away with a smile. And this was as good of time as any to share my first kiss with Braxton.

I loved Braxton, he was such a God fearing and let's forget a father fearing man which canceled every inappropriate thought he might have had about me. But, I think a good bye kiss would be acceptable in God's sight, even if my father disagreed.

I still had one school year before I could join Braxton at the same college. All I could think about was me and him starting a student ministry on campus led by Braxton and I would attend all of his home basketball games. I was so excited that God was laying my steps out one by one.

Pastor Clemons was driving Braxton to the airport alone. I think they needed to have their last father and son, stay saved talk. The car was loaded. Braxton gave his little brother so dap and threw an elbow at him. They always seem to joke around like that. Braxton hugged his mother so tight; he lifted her off the ground.

As soon as her feet hit land again, his mother signaled his brother to come in the house and Pastor Clemons got in the car. I guess this was their way of letting us say goodbye in private. Braxton hugged me, and kissed the top of my head that was barely at his chest. That was not what I was expecting but I'll take it. After letting me go Braxton sprinted to the car and waved goodbye as they pulled out of the driveway.

Church wasn't the same with Braxton gone, but it gave me the opportunity to practice becoming a first lady. Braxton loved his mother about as much as he loved Jesus, so if I acted like her, he would love me the same and make me his first lady. Besides, there is no better way to get in than being co-signed by somebody's momma.

The best way for me to be fashioned into a first lady was to become Lady Clemon's amour bearer. Not only would I gain the secrets that could be shared behind the veil, I would know how to marry the man of my dreams and stay married for over 25 years.

I watched everything that the first lady did. I copied her mannerisms, her style, and her dialect. I decided to do everything just like her. She became my idol. You know what I mean not really idol as in pagan worship, but she was the person that I needed to pattern my life after. I knew that I would be in perfect standing with Braxton and ready to come off the bench as Mrs. Braxton Clemons, First Lady of Savior Missionary Baptist Church.

I kept myself busy at church and at school while Braxton was away at college. I kept up with him mostly online. He was at Syracuse on a full ride scholarship. The team was doing very well. I was cheering for them to win every game but secretly I had hoped they would lose so that Braxton would get to come home for Christmas break. If Syracuse advanced to the playoffs, there would be no Christmas for anybody this year. Low and behold, Syracuse made it all the way.

Things were not going like they should. First Braxton didn't come home for Christmas then my father informed me that since I didn't get a scholarship at Syracuse, I would have to attend state school. Then to top it all off, it was my senior prom and I was the bell of the ball without a date. I had never dated anyone but Braxton so my options were null and void. But I was ok with that. Braxton was worth saving myself for.

Summer was here, my first taste of freedom. I was out of high school, grown, and driving. My parents bought me a car for graduation. I had a new car but nowhere to go. Braxton's momma told me that he went to a camp for the summer and was not going to come home at all. It was a long, hot, miserable summer without seeing Braxton.

I was preparing to head off to college and it had been a year since I had seen Braxton, but my college was just a couple hours away from home so whenever he got home, I would be able to see him. I still kept in contact with Braxton between classes, his games, and homework. But, the second verse was same as the first.

Braxton did not come home for Christmas. He was playing better than he had in high school and once again everybody was talking about a pro career was inevitable for him. But I knew that God had a greater plan for Him and God always has the last word. I had a dream that Braxton was elevated to the office of Bishop. As he preached, I was by his side, with his parents there as honorees.

I was enjoying being on my own and I was getting used to college. I met two amazing women of God their names were Cassie and Alicia. They weren't saved but I was there to lead them to Christ. They were at every party, they knew all the latest styles, but they didn't know the Lord as their personal savior. Greater is He that is in me than he that is in the world, so they would definitely become saved.

One afternoon, I was sitting in the lounge with Cassie and Alicia watching the game. I made them watch it with me because Braxton was playing. Of course, they won. God's favor rested on him. During the postgame interview I noticed there was a girl that seemed pretty chummy with Braxton.

I knew the groupies would come out the woodwork since he announced last week that he was going to enter the draft. She couldn't wait to get on camera.

"Do ya'll see that Jezebel hoe hanging on my man?"

"I hate to tell you Braxton is not your man. He is about to go pro. He doesn't want some plain Jane church girl on his arm, when he can have his pick of the litter." Cassie said with a slight chuckle.

"Whatever, I know his parent's won't approve of him being with a girl that don't know the Lord."

"You don't know nothing about that girl, you don't even know if that is his girl much less, if she goes to church. Sit down, go pray or something."

"I can see through that Mac and Mary Kay. She has no idea what to do with a man like Braxton."

I refused to listen to them. They are my friends, but I can't talk to carnal people about spiritual matters. Later that evening I tried to call Braxton but he wasn't there. I wanted to pray with him. I wasn't able to get him on the phone and he didn't call me back. This was not like Braxton, but I knew that God's hedge of protection surrounded him.

I was so excited. Lady Clemons told me that Braxton was coming home. This was going to be my first time seeing him in about two years. After I went home to see my parents, I made a beeline to the Clemon's house. My excitement was quenched when I walked into the family room to see Braxton on the couch hugged up with the girl that I saw him with on TV. Braxton saw me and jumped off the couch.

"There's my girl. What's up? I miss you girl." Braxton said as he gave me a bear hug lifting me off the ground. I was caught up in the moment that I forgot all about the girl sitting on there. She didn't budge; I guess she knew her place. When Braxton let me go he said,

"Stacy come here, I want you to meet Myra. We basically grew up together; she is the sister I never had. Myra this is Stacy, my fiancée."

That was not what I was expecting to hear. I extended my hand to shake her hand.

"Girl, we almost family, we can't shake hands; you have to hug my neck. Praise God I finally get to meet you. I have heard so much about you."

What is really going on here? This is a bit overwhelming. Braxton has went to college, got a fiancée, and did she just say praise the Lord? I couldn't help but be cordial and give her a hug and pretend I was happy to meet her too.

"It is nice to meet you too Stacy. Where are you from?"

"I was born and raised in Oklahoma. My parents still live there. They have a pretty nice size congregation, but I had to get out of there. I needed to spread my wings and see what direction God wanted me to go. Instead of always having people in my ear telling me what God told them about me. I have to tell them. God ain't gonna give you a word about me or for me without giving it to me first. My destiny is greater than being the praise team leader."

Lady Clemons walked back in the room with some refreshments.

"Myra, Stacy sings like an angel. I can't wait for you to hear her sing at church on Sunday."

I'm trying to figure out what I missed. How did I move from lady in waiting to family? And, Lady Clemons usually have better discernment than this. Just because Stacy throws out a couple things about God and the church doesn't means that she is saved. Satan knows the word of God too.

I was able to fake it until I made it out of there. I was not trying to be Stacy's friend. She was only a distraction. She was supportive of Braxton leaving college to go play in the pros. That is not God's plan for his life.

Although Braxton was home, I didn't get to see him much. With him entering the draft there were agents, reporters, fans, family, and groupies everywhere. Every time I looked up he was either going to or coming from a meeting.

The big day had finally come. The NBA draft was here. Pastor Clemons decided to let the whole church watch it together in the fellowship hall. The official announcement was made. Braxton Clemons was a third-round draft pick and was heading to play for Houston. Everyone cheered.

Braxton was hailed as a hometown hero. I think the entire world has watching the draft. I only saw it as picking teams like we did on the playground when we were little. I wish I knew something about sports, that way I could truly be excited for him.

The way I saw it he will still be doing what he's been doing since I think he was in like the sixth grade. I was surprised to hear from Cassie, she called to make sure I was alright. I was ok with what was going on, but I was so sad that the Clemons bought into the mess. Stacy may call herself Braxton's fiancée, but that would soon come to an end so that I could take my rightful place in his life.

Braxton was coming home for the summer. This was our last chance to spend time together before he moved to Houston. I enjoyed being home to visit my parents but to actually have someone to hang out with was exciting. Cassie had an internship this summer and Alicia was traveling with her family. So that meant I had plenty of time to spend with Braxton.

The phone rang. I was happy to see that it was the Clemons' residence. Braxton was calling me first. I didn't have to make the first move. With excitement I said,

"Hello."

"Hello daughter, this is 1st Lady Clemons, how are you today?"

"I'm good ma'am, how are you today."

"I'm blessed and highly favored of the Lord. Can you meet me at the church house in about an hour I need you to help me out with a few things."

"Yes ma'am, I will see you in an hour."

I wondered why she wanted me to come to the church; I just did what I was asked to do. When I got to the church, there were a couple of ladies that I didn't know walking around the sanctuary with Lady Clemons. I didn't know who they were. We just remodeled the church a couple years ago so they couldn't be decorators. They were carrying books, material, a camera and all kinds of stuff.

"Hello Lady Clemons, I'm here."

"Hey baby, come on and follow us, we were just heading back into the office."

I headed towards the ladies and followed them to the church office. Lady Clemons began introductions.

"Ladies, this is Myra, she is not just my daughter in the Lord, her and Braxton have been like brother and sister long as I could remember."

Ok when did we become brother and sister? We went to prom together, we were dating, but why is she telling these strangers this? I thought.

"Myra this is Laura and Phyllis. Laura is Stacy's sister and Phyllis is her auntie."

We all smiled and exchanged pleasantries before we sat down. Stacy lived in Oklahoma, why were her people in Colorado? I'm tripping, it is almost time to start planning our Annual Women's Conference one of them must be coming to speak. Lady Clemons started talking.

"Let's get started. Myra, Laura and Ms. Phyllis are here to help plan the wedding. Since we have less than 30 days, they decided to fly out for about a week or so to get things in order. Braxton and Stacy are going to get married here instead of in Oklahoma. I've assigned you as the point person to get them any help that they need."

I nodded my head in agreement; they were really going forward with this wedding. Only what God puts together will last forever so I don't know why everyone is making a big deal about this. I sat through the meeting scarcely listening to the details. I was still in shock. It seemed like we were meeting for hours, when I looked at the clock not even an hour had passed. I just needed to go home. The meeting was dismissed, and I said goodbye to everyone.

I drove home to my mother sitting on the patio. When she saw me, she stood up and said.

"Baby, I'm sorry come here let me give you a hug."

"Momma the devil is busy." I said as I rested my head in my mother's bosom.

"I wanted to be the one to tell you that Braxton was marrying that girl before he moves to Houston but you were sleep when I left and gone when I got back."

My mom and I sat down next to each other.

"Why momma, everybody knows that we were supposed to get married and work together in ministry, why?"

"I know that you thought Braxton was your husband. I didn't know how to tell you. I thought you would eventually grow out of that puppy love."

"Momma it is more that puppy love. It was prophesied to me."

"I know you know your Bible; it says we prophesy in part. And, you never asked for revelation of the word that you received. Sometimes people tell us things just to encourage us."

"You've seen how good we are together, tell me that ain't God? I patterned my life after Lady Clemons to show that I can be a first lady."

"I'm not saying that it ain't God, I'm saying that you and Braxton are not meant to be."

I could not believe what my mother was telling. She out of all people is supposed to understand and support me.

"Myra listen to your momma baby, a man wants a wife. He doesn't want to marry his mother. When you chose to be like his mother instead of being yourself, he stopped looking at you and could only see his mother. You have your positional picked out but have you ever asked Braxton does he want to be in ministry fulltime? Have you ever made your feelings known to him?"

"No I just assumed everybody knew God's plan."

"Myra you are beautiful, be yourself. You dress and carry yourself like an old church mother. It's ok to wear jeans and to put on some makeup. There is more to being saved than just looking like it."

"I'm going to go take a nap. Call me when dinner is ready."

"Smile baby, God will never give us more than we can handle."

I continued to my room. I just laid in my bed, stared at the ceiling and talked to God. I needed all of His grace and mercy to get me through the next several weeks. Working with Laura and Ms. Phyllis, I served them as if I was serving the Lord himself. We managed to pull off an almost perfect wedding.

It would have been perfect if Braxton had chosen me as his bride. The new Mr. and Mrs. Braxton Clemons were headed to Houston to begin their life together. I sent them away with a smile and best wishes.

For the next few years, I sat waiting to watch the devil reveal himself in their marriage. But it seemed like year after year. Braxton and Stacy grew happier and happier. Braxton's NBA career was flourishing and after about two years together, the children started coming. I never gave up hope. I wanted children of my own but I can settle with being a stepmother. I would love them as if they were my own, since I loved Braxton so much.

After the wedding, I never talked about Braxton to anyone. No one understood that he was sacred to my heart, and no one was going to convince me that we weren't destined to be together. I will just wait on the Lord and keep myself holy.

Each year Braxton brought his family home to Denver during the off season. Braxton tried to act like nothing between us had changed, but something was different. Hello, he had a whole wife, and I no longer had a rightful place at the table. I made myself scarce because I was tired of having the scab ripped off my wound over and over again by being invited to family dinners and listening to Stacy and her, *"my husband this, my husband that."* For heaven's sake does she know any other word besides husband?

After about four or five years, it seemed as though the assignment of the enemy was beginning to crumble. For whatever reason Braxton was not getting any playing time and there was no talk about him being traded to another team. That meant, if he wasn't playing ball anymore, that gold diggin' hoochie he married would surely divorce him and we can move forward with our life together.

I continued to serve at the church because I knew I needed to be prepared and in position to be Braxton's wife. I was the armor bearer to Braxton's mom, worked as the church administrator, and sang on the praise team. I was at the church at least three days a week and got to know Pastor Clemons very well.

This particular Sunday, Pastor Clemons seemed to be in unusually good spirits. He had taken Jesus Joy to a whole new level. He paraded through the church before service like a peacock showcasing its feathers.

"Pastor, why are you strutting around the church this morning?" I asked.

"In due season daughter, in due season."

Pastor Clemons remarked as he walked back into his office. I didn't know what was about to happen but, I know the Lord is faithful.

Sunday morning service progressed as usual. Pastor could barely sit still in the pulpit. I was really trying to figure out what had him so gitty. He wasn't this excited when Braxton was drafted in the NBA. Finally, Pastor stepped to the microphone to preach. He signaled for Lady Clemons to join him at his side. He hugged his wife and kissed her on top of her head before he grabbed her by the hand and began to speak.

"Well as everybody knows I have been the senior pastor of this church for over 20 years. My wife and I have raised our kids, and some of ya'll too. I've seen the goodness of Jesus multiply year after year. Just when I thought He couldn't do nothing else, He shows up and shows that He is God and God alone and because of that, I have decided to step down as Senior Pastor."

I was not alone when I felt like this was a gut punch. This was not what I was expecting him to say. Who was going to be our new Pastor? The congregation of people stood up murmured and became restless. No one was ready to say good bye to the man of God. Pastor Clemons signaled to everyone to be seated so he could continue.

"This is a joyous day. The Bible says that your latter days will be greater than your former. And, there is no better way to enjoy my latter days than to travel with my wife. We are about to get reacquainted with each other before we get too old to enjoy each other. And, glory to God, the mantle that is on me, is being passed on to my very son.

Braxton will be elevated to the office of Senior Pastor. I will still be around to make sure he learned what I taught him. He and his family will be moving back to Denver to continue to advance the kingdom of God. He has decided to retire from the NBA after this season.

Over the next several months things will be prepared for a smooth transition. The Bible said train up a child in the way he should go and when he grows old he will not depart from it. And, I am a witness to that. Despite the fame and fortune Braxton has never forsaken the Lord.

My soul began to rejoice. The man that was promised to be my husband was finally coming home to be with me. About time, I was wearing myself out trying to keep busy. I can't wait to see him. Alicia will not be the only married one anymore. Braxton and I should be ready to get married in about a year. I just want a small, simple wedding. When you are really in love you don't have to put on a production for the world.

I was so excited that Braxton was coming back that I couldn't tell anyone. I wanted to surprise everyone with the announcement of my wedding. I know for sure as soon as Braxton makes the announcement that he is leaving the NBA, that Ms. Thang of a wife will cast him aside to search for the next number one draft pick. Then, Braxton will finally find his favor with the Lord through me.

Over the next several months, the kids and Stacy began to make more and more frequent trips back to Denver without Braxton for extended periods of time. I guess she was planning her exit strategy. She was living with Pastor 'nem, which was a little odd to me. I guess she wasn't planning to make Colorado her home.

The wait was finally over; Braxton was coming home for good. His life as a professional ball player finally ended.

There was such a praise in my heart. The Lord will never leave me or forsake me. Lady Clemons called me a few days after Braxton arrived. She asked me to come help her and Stacy pack up. You know I jumped on that opportunity; I was more than happy to bid Stacy and her stuff good bye.

I arrived at the Clemons' home, there was a truck out front and movers everywhere. I walked in with the biggest grin on my face. There was nothing that the devil could do to still my joy.

"Hello everyone." I said as I walked through the door. Stacy was the very first person to greet me as I walked in.

"Thank you so much Myra for coming to help out. Braxton was right you are truly an angel."

I'm glad she recognized who she was dealing with. I smiled as I hugged her.

"No problem, what do you need help with?"

"Well, the men have already loaded the truck with the little bit of stuff we had here so we're just going over to the house to unpack and get everything situated. You know men, they are bound to bring the stuff inside the house and just sit it in the middle of the floor."

I was a little confused about what she just said. I didn't understand where the movers were coming from or whose house they were taking the stuff to. I had to ask for more details.

"That's fine. Whose house are we moving the stuff to?"

"Oh girl I'm sorry, I thought you knew. Braxton had a house out south, built from the ground up for us. It was supposed to be finished months ago but they got delayed with this crazy Colorado weather. That is why the kids and I have been staying here. But everything happens for a reason. The kids had time to spend with their grandparents. Ok, let's get started."

What the hell! I can't believe that she is really trying to stay here. I don't think she understands that there is a huge difference between being an NBA wife and a Pastor's wife. I just nodded my head a followed her.

We loaded up and went to this mini mansion. I was impressed, this house was huge. Braxton and the men were getting everything inside. After parking my car, I yelled at Braxton,

"Let the men work, you know you don't know nothing about physical labor."

He walked towards me with the biggest smile. He put his arm around me, chuckled and said,

"That is what I keep trying to tell my wife, but it seems like my *honey do* list keeps getting longer and longer. Thanks for helping out. Having you around always brightens my day. I love you girl. Come in and let me give you the nickel tour of the house."

See I knew I wasn't crazy. He loved me just like I loved him. I was eager to see what would eventually be my home. Walking in onto marble floors and a winding staircase everything was just like I had always imagined. I had a vision of me standing on top of the staircase in a long silk night gown, welcoming Braxton home. I vividly saw myself being queen of this castle. After putting in several hours of labor, I finally had enough.

"Well, Ms. Stacy. I'm gonna get out of here. If you need more help, let me know and I will come back over later this week."

"You have been a true blessing. I can handle things from here. I appreciate your time. Do you need some gas money or something?"

"I would not dream of accepting any money from you. Consider it a seed. God bless you, see you guys at church."

I could not wait to tell Alicia about my day. I called her from the car.

"Hey lady, what are you doing?"

"Nothing, Arlington took the kids somewhere so I'm just enjoying my peaceful house. What are you doing?"

"You will never believe what I got to tell you. Why have I spent my entire day helping Braxton and his wife move into their brand new custom built home?"

"Because you're crazier than I thought you were."

"Stop, I'm being serious. You already heard that Braxton retired from the NBA, well I didn't tell you that he has been appointed as Senior Pastor and it won't be too long before he's Bishop. You know that Jezebel of a wife of his is not ready to be a First Lady. That means, my wait has not been in vain, I am finally about to get my husband."

"I hope you are right. You have been waiting all of your whole life for this man. I hope he is worth it."

"Delight yourself in the Lord and he will give you the desires of your heart."

"Let me cut you off before you get started. You and Ms. Shirley kill me trying to take people to church on days other than Sunday."

"Alicia the church is in you."

"Ok, hail Mary three times and whatever, I know this is not why you called me."

"I need your help. I trust in the Lord but sometimes He moves too slow for me. I need to light a fire under Stacy so she can hurry up and get her some ghost and I don't mean the Holy Ghost."

"Now you're speaking my language. This is going to be a little hard to stomach but, all you have to do is make your presence known. Keep working at the church and every time the doors open be there and be helpful. Make her your best friend. If I was you, I would even become her assistant so that I could sit behind her. Every time Braxton looks up at her, he will see you. Remind him that you are all that."

For once, Alicia was actually giving some me some sound advice. The devil can't stand the presence of God. With me present, the devil, I mean Stacy, was sure to flee.

"Thanks Alicia, you said exactly what I needed to hear. I will keep you posted on the progress. But in the meantime, you might want to iron your sea foam green, taffeta dress."

"You finally marrying Braxton will be an answer to your prayers. Getting me in a sea foam green anything would be the work of the devil."

Alicia and I spent time on the phone devising my plan and how to execute it. I needed to make sure I was wise as a fox and as cunning as a serpent. If anyone else knew what I was doing they may have misunderstood my motives, but God knows my heart is in the right place.

Braxton's role at the church became more and more prevalent. As changes were being made, I played my part. Rumors began to surface that Braxton would be elevated to the office of Bishop within the next year or so. I tried not to have a lustful heart, but hearing Braxton preach and hearing how his gift developed over the years only made me want him more.

It seemed like everything was moving along as planned until, Stacy showed up out the clear blue sky at choir rehearsal. The Minister of Music had her lead most of the songs that we were learning. I was the praise team leader. Just because she was the Pastor's wife, she did not have the right or authority to take charge of anything. This was something that I would definitely have to address with Pastor; Stacy was most certainly out of order.

Being cast into the role Alicia asked me to play was not cutting it. She said grin and barer it, but I had to do something different because my patience was wearing thin. Braxton didn't treat me any different from the other leaders at the church. That meant I wasn't standing out enough, time to pull out the big guns.

I finally had the opportunity to lead a song at church. I decided to sing one of me and Braxton's golden oldies. I started singing the song. Braxton grabbed his microphone and joined in with me on time and in key. He really sang the song. The spirit of the Lord filled the church. This was my doorway in. Braxton handed the mic to Stacy and transformed our song into a two-part harmony. How dare she rain on my parade? I continued the duet with her because I didn't want to show how upset I was. But to add insult to injury at the conclusion of the song Braxton wrapped his arm around Stacy and said,

"Ya'll give it up for my wife. Ain't God good? He blessed me with one of His very own angels. She really ministered that song."

He kissed Stacy and moved forward with service, giving me no recognition at all. Why did Stacy think it was ok to steal my thunder? It was obvious that she was trying to outdo me. As Stacy headed past me back to her seat she whispered,

"Let it go, God never promised you, my husband. I got this."

I looked at her in silence because she didn't know what she was talking about, and she really didn't know who she was talking to. I made it up in my mind to have a conversation with Braxton after service.

"Braxton, I mean Pastor. I think we need to have a talk about Stacy. I believe she has an issue with me. I don't feel she respects me. She just got to this church, and she is trying to take over everything that I do. You need to talk to her about protocol."

Braxton turned and stared at me as if he was confused. He then took a couple steps towards me. I know he will check her or anybody when it comes to me.

"Myra, all I am gonna say to you is Stacy is the first lady, my wife, and you will respect her as such. Anything that she says or does is in alignment with my vision. My wife does not carry the spirit of Jezebel, and I pray you don't either. You are not married to this church or me for the fact of the matter. I appreciate you serving the church but it's time for you to get a life. I mean it! Quit hiding in the church and let your husband find you. Have a blessed day."

Braxton sat down behind his desk and began to do some paperwork. Stacy really had him fooled. That's ok; I know the devil ain't got no patience. I will keep myself holy and pure for the day that Braxton and I become one. I walked out of his office aborting Alicia's plan and put it in God's hands.

Checkmate

My family was back on track. Things between Arlington and I were better than they had ever been. We seemed to be laughing again and communicating rather than just talking. I hate to admit it but, Piper was the best thing to ever happen to my marriage. The kids and I were settled back into our home and my fairytale life had become reality.

I left the office early because the kids didn't have school. It was such a beautiful day. The sun was shining brightly, and it was a mild breeze blowing. Rather than taking the kids to the park, I decided to let them play in front of the house. I watched AJ and Ariah ride their bikes up and down the driveway to the corner and back again. I enjoy spending time with the kids but this was a little boring. I thought to myself, I might as well get some work done while I'm just sitting here.

"Kids, I'm going inside to grab my laptop and stuff, I'll be right back. Do not go in the street."

"Yes, mom. They responded in unison.

It seemed like no sooner than I grabbed my briefcase and headed back outside, I heard tires screeching. As my briefcase fell off my shoulder, my heart dropped. I ran outside to see AJ lying in the street crying with his mangled bike next to him. Oh my God, I could not believe that this was happening. One of my neighbors saw what happened. As she headed over to me, she yelled,

"The police are on the way. Is AJ ok?"

"Thank you. There isn't any blood, but I better take him to the emergency room just in case."

AJ was crying and wasn't trying to get off the ground.

"Son, tell mommy where it hurts?"

"My leg hurts, and I bumped my head too. It hurts mommy."

I was a nervous wreck. This was the last thing I needed right now. Hearing Piper's story a few months ago, made me realize how fragile life was and I was not going to let my son pay the price for my carelessness. My heart was pounding so loud, that I could barely think. Instead of waiting for the police, I put AJ in the truck and decided to drive him to the hospital myself. I needed God to step into this situation for me. I called Myra so she could meet me at the hospital. Without a second thought, Myra said she was walking out the door.

When I arrived at the hospital Myra was already there, she grabbed Ariah as I carried AJ inside. He had stop crying but I was still scared that something was really wrong with him. Once I got AJ back into a room to be examined by the doctor I called Arlington.

"Arlington, come to Mercy General right away, AJ was hit by a car on his bike."

"Is he ok? Alicia tell me that my son is alright."

"I don't know for sure, I will fill you in on what happened when you get here." My voice was shaking but I managed to speak without crying hysterically.

"Calm down, I'm on my way."

I was so glad Arlington and I were back together. I could not imagine going through this alone. I knew AJ was going to recover from this accident, but I was still so worried. All I could do is sit and rock back and forth. This was one time that I was glad Myra was there. She walked the floor praying. I knew if nothing else, God heard her prayers.

This was one time; I really hoped Jesus was on the main line. Although Arlington was there in 15 minutes, it felt like a lifetime had passed before he arrived. When Arlington walked through the door, he was a sight for sore eyes. He came through the doors as if he was out of breath.

"What happened? Where is AJ?" I recognized the fear that he had in his eyes.

"The kids were riding their bikes in the cul-de-sac. A car was speeding around the corner; before we knew it AJ was hit. The car knocked him off his bike and kept going. I left before the police got there, but I left my card with the neighbor. She saw everything so she can tell the police what happened better than I can. The police haven't checked in with me yet to let me know what's going on. They still have AJ in x-ray so I can't tell you how bad he is yet."

I fell into Arlington's arms and just cried. The kids and I had only been home for a couple of months, I was not going to let a tragedy tear my family apart again. Since Arlington had shown up, Myra decided to take Ariah with her so we could focus on AJ without scaring her. Having my head resting on Arlington's chest was so comforting but I still couldn't keep my mind from thinking about the worst case scenario. My heart still hadn't stopped racing.

"Alicia, I promise everything is going to be alright."
I knew Arlington was scared too, but he made sure he stood strong for me. Times like this made me remember why I married him. I found new reasons to love him every day.

Arlington loosened the hold he had on me, so I looked up to see the doctor heading towards us.

"Dr. Kenard, this is Arlington my husband. Honey, this is the AJ's doctor."

"Mr. Rowe it's a pleasure to meet you. Well guys you have a champion, your son is going to be all right, he has a concussion and a broken leg but everything else looks good. We are about to take him into surgery to reset that leg. There may be some internal bleeding because his blood pressure is low. If that is the case, we might have to give him a transfusion."

"Dr. Kenard, is there a way that either my wife or I could give the transfusion? You know with AIDS and everything I would feel better if he had blood from one of us."

"Ok, go to the nurse's station and someone will direct you guys to the lab. I will check in with you after surgery."

Even with going to the lab to donate blood, it seemed that time was dragging its feet. Myra called and checked in as she headed out to Bible study. She assured me that she would make sure she lifted us up in prayer. Arlington cuddled me, periodically kissing my forehead as we sat in silence hoping and wishing that our son would recover completely. This was confirmation that I married the right man, and the love we shared was worth all of the ups and downs that we have endured.

Two long hours had passed and Dr. Kenard finally appeared. Both Arlington and I stood up.

"Mr. and Mrs. Rowe, your champion is heading to a complete recovery. I was able to set the bone and we didn't need the transfusion after all. I want to keep him for a couple days just to play it safe. He will be back to riding his bike before you know it." Arlington shook Dr. Kenard's hand.

"Thank you so much doctor, you are a lifesaver. We appreciate your efforts."

"You're welcome that's why I make the big bucks. By the way, for future reference, you might want to have your son's father have a supply of blood on hand if don't want blood from a stranger."

"Doctor, my husband gave blood today also."

"I know, but your son's blood types don't match either one of you, and I know dealing with an ex can be difficult but, his biological father has to be the donor."

"Excuse me doctor, I am AJ's father, his biological father, are you sure you have the right file?"

"Yes, your son's name is Arlington Rowe Jr. correct, date of birth September 12, 2003?"

"Yeah, but I don't understand?"

Arlington looked at Dr. Kenard then at me. I looked towards the doctor. With a concerning yet confused look Dr. Kenard said,

"I apologize, I didn't know. Maybe I should leave the two of you alone to talk. The nurse will notify you when you can go to see your son in recovery."

Dr. Kenard walked away, I was paralyzed. I didn't know what to say or do. I knew Arlington was heated. I watched while his countenance changed. I swear I saw all the blood rush to his face and steam flow from his ears, like I've seen in the cartoons. Arlington stared out the window for what seemed like an eternity. He rubbed his hand over his head and walked towards me. I've never been so scared in my life, my eyes bulged and my palms were sweaty.

Arlington had never been violent before, but I thought he was going to choke me right here in the hospital. Instead, he slammed his fist against the wall behind me. Arlington looked at me with such rage.

"Don't say shit to me." He said as he glared and walked away.

Oh my God, I didn't know what to do. More importantly, I didn't know what Arlington was about to do.

The one secret I held so deep inside my heart that I never thought about finally reared its ugly head with vengeance. No one knew the truth about my son. I was too embarrassed to tell anyone that there was a possibility that Arlington wasn't my son's father. But nothing short of the move of God and an act of congress would be able to help me out of this mess. I stood in one place with a million thoughts running through my mind. Finally, my blank stare was interrupted by the nurse letting me know that I could go in and see AJ.

There were tubes and machines crowding my son. His left leg was propped up in a cast. The tears rolled down my face. My baby was lying in a hospital bed and I was standing over him alone.

I had no idea what I would tell him when he asked for his father. AJ barely opened his eyes. He slowly lifted his arm to reach out to me. Tears began to swell in my eyes and a single tear dropped.

"Momma, don't cry. Daddy will buy me another bike, if my old one is broken." I couldn't help but chuckle at my son. He just experienced major surgery and all he could think about was his bike. I pulled the chair next to the bed and held his hand.

"Hey son, I love you so much."

"I love you to momma. Don't be sad, I'll get another bike."

Before, I could respond AJ had shut his eyes again. As the nurse checked the machines, she noticed the concerned look on my face as AJ shut his eyes.

"He's ok, his vital signs are good. The anesthesia hasn't worn off and the trauma of the accident will probably cause him to sleep for the rest of the night. Sleep is how the body heals itself. You can either stay here or go home but he won't be able to communicate with you until tomorrow."

"Thank you so much. I am so worried about him."

"No need to worry. My name is Suzie and I will be his nurse for the next 12 hours. I will be in here every hour to check on him, so if you need anything or choose to stay the night just let me know."

"Suzie I appreciate that. I'm going to hang out for a while. I will let you know if I change my mind about staying."

Everyone seemed to show up at the hospital at the same time. My parents, Cassie, and Myra brought balloons and cards for AJ. Ariah even colored a picture for her big brother.

"Where's Arlington?" Myra asked. I couldn't tell anyone what happened without telling on myself. I was not ready to confess to anyone that I really didn't know who my son's father was after all of these years.

"You just missed him. He left the office so abruptly when I called him that he had to go back and tie up a few loose ends. He should be on his way back in about an hour or so."

Everyone seemed to have bought the lame excuse, but I had to figure out something very soon. There is no way that I could keep the charade up very long. Everyone was comforting me and reaffirming that AJ was alright, not that I don't love my son but AJ was the least of my concerns right now.

It was getting late, and AJ still hadn't opened his eyes, everyone started to leave. My parents took Ariah with them so I could at least focus on what to do. I needed to go too, but where would I go. Home was not an option. I have never seen Arlington so enraged, and I was not trying to say or do the wrong thing to set him off. I considered calling him but, I'm sorry didn't seem appropriate right now.

I decided to take the path of least resistance and went to Ms. Shirley's house. Although I hated what she had to say sometimes, I knew she would at least point me in the right direction. Her house was not only a safe haven but her kitchen table was one place where I could be transparent and meditate on any situation.

Ms. Shirley must have seen me drive up, because the porch light came on and the front door opened as I got out of my truck.

"Girl, it has gotten chilly out here. Come on in before you catch cold." I headed inside her house, straight to the kitchen.

"Ms. Shirley I need you. I have really messed up this time. I am about to lose everything that I know and love. I know you don't think I listen to you but I do and I need you. I'm too embarrassed to talk to anyone else."

"Chile, it can't be that bad, tell me what's going on. AJ is going to be alright quit worrying and let God have his way."

"Ms. Shirley I wish it was that simple. AJ is going to be alright, it's his father that is the problem."

"I know that you and Arlington have been having problems, but I am positive that he wouldn't jeopardize his son's life in order prove a point to you. Cut the man some slack ya'll just got back together, don't go accusing him of nothing."

"Arlington is not AJ's father."

"What are you talking about girl?"

"I am about to tell you something that no one but God knows. I met Arlington at the club and hit it off immediately. He said he never thought he would meet a good woman like me. He begged me to have his baby. And see, he had some tickets and stuff from his DUI, that he had to get cleared up that is why we didn't meet each other's family's until after the baby was born."

Ms. Shirley was up making a pot of coffee, but she turned towards me with both hands on her hips and said,

"Listen to me little girl, let me stop you right here. Don't try to feed me a bunch of mess. If you want me to help you, you got to tell me the truth. The for real truth."

"I am telling you the truth. You cut me off before I had a chance to tell you my story."

"That's what I am saying, don't tell me a story. Tell me the truth. If what you're telling me is true, then you gotta be the biggest fool alive. I know a man will say anything to get a piece of ass, but baby you cannot convince me that after only seeing you in the club and having sex with you, Arlington thought you were a good woman. He didn't think you were worth meeting the people that were important and he didn't mention marriage, but he wanted you to have his baby. Child, I'm old but not crazy. I can go to bed now and get my share of drama when I watch the soaps in the morning. I can't tell you what to do, if you don't tell me the truth."

I looked at Ms. Shirley's face. I knew she meant business and I needed to come clean.

"You're right, I was a fool. But it wasn't Arlington's fault. I made a fool of myself. I should say it was Cassie and Myra's fault, they told me anything worth having is worth working for and I was the type of woman that he needed in his life because-"

Before I could finish my sentence, Ms. Shirley interrupted.

"There is a difference between an opinion and advice. An opinion is based upon emotion and influenced by experience. Advice is based upon facts and is executed with wisdom. But in either case, if you don't tell the truth or the whole story you will get incomplete or inaccurate council. I'm not here to judge you. I'm here to do what you asked me to do which is help."

"You're right. I guess somebody needs to know the truth. I was never Arlington's girlfriend, but I was in love with him and was willing to do anything to get him. When I met him, he was 32, with no kids, and ran the streets 3 or 4 days a week. I felt if I gave him the one thing no one else had given him he would be mine. I knew having a baby would make a difference in his life." Ms. Shirley interrupted again,

"Is this really coming from *Ms. Things Have Changed Since Your Day*? Because back in my day a man would marry you if you were in the family way, a man would make an honest woman out of you. That doesn't happen anymore. Men today treat the mother of their kids like she ain't family. But it looks like you snagged a good one and it worked."

"No ma'am. Actually, it didn't work. He denied the baby was his."

"How on earth did you get yourself in this situation? If you got pregnant on purpose, why isn't Arlington AJ's father?"

"Well Ms. Shirley, when I met Arlington, he gave me so much attention. He was tall, fine, and he made me laugh. Everybody told me to leave him alone because he was just a hoe, he was sorry, and a drunk. But, I couldn't help myself. No one ever made me feel like he did."

"I need to understand, what did you feel that was so earth shattering? Did you have anything outside the club and bed, I don't think it was what you felt, it was where you felt it that convinced you to trap this man."

"This is such a mess I don't know where to begin."

"Well baby, just start talking."

"Cassie and I used to hang out at this hole in the wall bar called Starters. One night there was a group of guys hanging out taking pictures, talking smack, and drinking. Arlington caught my eye. We began flirting back and forth for a few weeks, but nothing ever happened. Until one night he was too drunk to drive, and he asked if I would take him home. I found him attractive, but I didn't plan on making a detour to my house. I have never had sex like that in my life. There was not an inch of my body that he left untouched. He made love to every part of my body, with such intimacy and passion. His touch was so gentle, and his caress was poetically smooth. Up this point I thought he was some fun-loving guy that I hung out with at the club, I never knew that this passionate, loving side of him existed. I have to say, this was the first time I ever made love."

Ms. Shirley was about to pour a cup of coffee, but she stopped, looked at me and shook her head.

"Never mind me baby, keep talking." She said.

"We made love all night long. I asked for his number and he gave it to me but he didn't come to the club or return my calls for a couple of weeks.

The truth of the matter is I believe he thought I was a one-night stand or he positioned me to be a one night stand. But, I knew what I felt was real and I could convince him that he was only single because I was the first good woman he had ever met. I knew that if I could just spend some time with him, he would recognize what we shared was more than a result of some drunken stupor. He showed up at the club after about a month and I asked if he wanted to go home with me and he did. The loving was as good as it was the first time."

I could not understand why Ms. Shirley was looking at me so surprised. She acted like she never heard of a woman openly admitting her feelings about sex.

"Ms. Shirley, you got something you want to say?"

"Naw baby, I'm just listening. Keep telling me what happened." With an attitude I continued.

"Anyway, I decided to push the envelope and tell Arlington how I felt. I know that I am a dime piece so he should be more than delighted to be seen with me in public. When I called to invite him to a movie and dinner, I even offered to pay.

Arlington had the nerve to tell me that he didn't want to go with me and that I was looking for more out of the relationship than what he was willing to give. I should have known then that he was intimidated by an independent black woman. The next couple of times I saw him out, he was acting funny and stuff, so I said the hell with him until, I found out that I was pregnant.

Now Ms. Shirley was looking confused. I felt like she was judging me, like I had something to be ashamed of. But I just kept talking.

"I had sex with my ex-boyfriend one time, when I was out of town on a business trip. But, I had my period before I had sex with Arlington again. I just knew he and I would be together. I was going to give him his first son. I was so excited about being pregnant. Everyone told me that I should get rid of the baby because Arlington was no good. But no one saw his potential. They did not see what I saw in him. I knew that I could bring the best out in him, especially if I had his baby."

Ms. Shirley looked at me like I was crazy as I kept talking.

"My plan backfired. At first, he thought I was lying about being pregnant. When I showed him the ultrasound of our son, he told me not to expect him to be excited or claim the baby until we got a blood test. I went through my whole pregnancy alone. He refused to talk to me, see me, and if I saw him in public he spoke and kept it moving. I couldn't admit the truth to myself so I made up lies about why he wasn't around. Arlington, seemed like a good man, I couldn't believe that he was acting like that."

Ms. Shirley sat down at the table and asked,

"What gave you the impression that he was a good man or capable of being a good father? You never did anything together but drink, laugh, and screw."

"You make it sound like I was just a bootie call."

"What else would you call it, when a man screws a woman and keeps her in hiding?"

"Everybody says behind every good man is a good woman. To me that meant that he hadn't met a good woman that would stand behind him and help him be a good man."

"Baby, you got that wrong, you can't help a man be a man, especially a good man. He has to know his purpose and have a sense of direction before he can be anything to anybody else. Most men that are not good men will not recognize a good woman anyway because he is not looking for one."

I knew Ms. Shirley was right, but it was too late now to try and correct what I had done. I know I should have listened to what everybody was saying but I needed to find out for myself. I guess I better continue with the story, I've come this far.

"When AJ was born, Arlington came to the hospital to see the baby, he never picked AJ up. He just looked at him and said call me when you are ready to take the blood test. AJ looked like me, but had light eyes just like Arlington. Even then, Arlington denied AJ was his son but against his wishes I named him Arlington Jr. because there was no doubt in my mind that Arlington was his father.

This was my momma's first grand baby, I couldn't tell her the truth and ruin things for her so I made up excuses of why Arlington wasn't around."

I was ashamed to keep talking to Ms. Shirley but I had to do whatever it took to get my family back on track.

"I remembered where Arlington's mother lived. I never met her, but I dropped him off there once to get his truck. Well, one day I got cute and dressed AJ up. I went over her house to introduce myself and AJ to her. Immediately she accepted AJ as her grandson. She never asked any questions about me and Arlington. She immediately started pulling out baby pictures of Arlington and calling people on the phone. When she called Arlington and ripped him a new one for not doing the right thing, he didn't reconsider his position at all. He was adamant about having nothing to do with me or AJ. Because his mother was so sure that AJ was her grandson a conversation about a blood test never came up again."

Ms. Shirley just nodded as I continued.

"Life was good other than the fact that Arlington only spent time with AJ if his mother had him. If I needed anything for the baby he would give his mother the money so she could go buy it. If I called Arlington he wouldn't pick up the phone, but would listen to my message then text me a response."

The coffee finally finished brewing. I added cream and sugar to the cup of coffee Ms. Shirley poured for me. After pouring herself a cup, she sat down at the table so I could finish the story.

"One day I saw Arlington with this chick named Avery or something like that. They were all hugged up and stuff. He tried to act like he was such a good dude so I went off! I cussed him out and told her that she was with a sorry ass nigga because he wasn't taking care of his son. Avery didn't say shit, sorry Ms. Shirley. But she didn't say nothing. Arlington tried to act hard and everything. Talking about because I clowned he could not and would not ever be with a woman like me. I knew he was just showing off for that chick. He knew he was glad to see me because I was looking good."

"Alicia, right there is your problem. You think everything hinges on the fact that you look good. Baby, I'm here to tell you, a man will choose an average looking good woman over a good looking average woman. If Arlington was interested in a relationship with you, you are showing out in public only pushed him further away. Everything you do, you should be a lady. And ladies don't go 'round cussing people out."

"He had it coming Ms. Shirley. He hadn't seen his son in two weeks but was out. I come to find out that he was living with her the whole time I was pregnant. That is why he couldn't be supportive. He was cheating on me."

"Do you hear yourself? Girl, you're making me nervous. If he was living with her and cattin' around town with you, then you were the sneaky, sneaky not her. I see you ain't learned nothing! That same mindset 'bout drove Arlington straight to Piper. And if you don't watch out, she still might get your husband."

For the life of me, I could never understand why Ms. Shirley always found something wrong with what I was doing. She is supposed to be on my side, my friend. Yet, she always took up for Arlington. But I guess, somebody gotta root for the underdog.

"I'm not gonna let you make me feel like I did something wrong. I was not gonna sit by and let him make me look like a fool. Everybody knew he was my baby daddy, but he was never with me and my son. That was not going down like that."

"You can't expect anybody to give you respect when you don't respect yourself. You never demanded him to take you out, show you off. Hell, quiet as its kept he was probably too embarrassed to take you any damn where you always cussing, fighting, and carry on. There's a worldly song that used to be out that said just because I'm wrong that don't make you right. If you understood just that phrase you would not be mad at Arlington so much. Baby the woman sets the climate in the relationship."

Ms. Shirley had that look in her eye. I know she was about to spit a couple of scriptures at me. I need to cut her off now. I will get a word when I get to church on Sunday, not today.

"Before you start in quoting the Bible, let me hurry up and tell you the rest so you can help me get my husband back home where he belongs."

"Go ahead since you know everything."

"He never told Avery about me or the baby, so I don't know what happened. I just know she put his sorry ass out. Well, this is where the plot thickens. One night I woke up to hear somebody pounding on my door. It was Arlington. He had been drinking like he always did on the weekends. I still don't know how he made it to my house as drunk as he was. Immediately after I let him in he passed out in my bed. I'll be damned if I sleep on the couch in my own house, so I laid down with him. Sometime during the night, I guess he realized where he was and that he missed me so we made love. Then we made love again the next morning. When he got out of bed he had a crazy look on his face, like he was frustrated that he was too drunk to really enjoy being with me for the first time in over a year."

"Lord knows, I can't follow your thought process. Honey, he was looking stupid in the face because he knew he just made a stupid mistake."

"I'm here to tell you and everybody else that God does not make mistakes. Because I got pregnant again, it was all a part of God's plan for us to be together as a family. That is why we got a boy and a girl."

"Don't blame that on God. He gave us free will and your will wasn't His will. God sanctified marriage, not dating, not sleeping together, and certainly not having babies because you ain't smart enough to use birth control."

"I always heard that God works in mysterious ways. So why can't this be one of His mysterious ways?"

"If you can show me that in the Bible, I will hold my peace. Child that ain't scripture. Until you stop doing weekly drive byes at the house of the Lord and get to know Him as your personal savior, don't go trying to quote His word because that is taking the Lord's name in vain."

I must have made Ms. Shirley angry because she raised her voice and tightened her lips. Let me reel her back in before she has a heart attack.

"I didn't come here to have Bible study. You got me all sidetracked. Ok, I said all that to say, that while we were at the hospital today me and Arlington gave blood just in case AJ needed a transfusion. Well, AJ's blood type didn't match mine or Arlington's so there is no way that he is Arlington's son. I knew that I had slept with someone else while I was dating Arlington, but I was positive that he was the father of my baby. As you can imagine Arlington is pretty pissed, he left the hospital without stopping by to see AJ in recovery."

"Have you talked to Arlington?"

"Nope, after my mom and everybody left the hospital and AJ went to sleep for the night, I came by here. I have no idea where he is at because his mother called to check on AJ on my way here. She's out of town this week."

"Before I tell you what I think, I need you to tell me what you want to happen."

"You already know what I want. I want my family to be back to normal. I want to move forward past today like it never happened. After all we just became a family again not too long ago. I believe AJ's accident was just to bring us closer together."

"I hate to be the one to tell you this, but that ain't about to happen. There is no way in the world Arlington is just gonna pretend that you haven't been lying to him for the past 6 years. That man feels betrayed, and he has every right to send you to where he found you."

"He should have got the blood test, if there was any doubt in his mind. Besides, all of this could have been avoided if he would've acknowledged his feelings and made a commitment to me from the jump."

"It's not Arlington's fault that you couldn't keep your legs closed long enough to get his attention. All you did was spark an interest in him. Maybe if you would have played hard to get, he would have been yours without all this devilment. But you don't want to take no responsibility for this situation; I ain't got nothing to say. You seem to have all the answers. Where do you plan to go from here? I suggest you ask your momma what to do, because I'm tired of talking to you."

"Now that ain't gonna happen. I'm not gonna talk to my momma. My momma is weak.

There is nothing she could tell me about relationships or a man. She found out my daddy was cheating on her and she didn't do anything about it. When she didn't leave him, I lost all respect for her."

"There is always more than what meets the eye. Your momma is a lot wiser than you think she is. People do things for different reasons. If you don't know the reasons, don't pass judgment."

"Well, you don't seem like you can help me, I guess I gotta figure this out on my own."

Ms. Shirley got up from the table and grabbed both of our cups of coffee, poured them out, and started making some dish water. I wondered what was going on, was she ignoring me or what? I just sat quiet for a minute to see if I needed to show myself out or what. After washing the 2 cups, she began to wipe off the table.

"Well, Ms. Shirley I have made a complete mess of things, but Arlington really loves me, and he loves the kids more so I know beyond a shadow of doubt he won't leave me before the kids are grown."

"There is another option, you can spend the next 13 years proving your love, your worth, and rebuilding the trust with your husband that YOU broke, and maybe, just maybe you will find that true love that you lost within your husband for real."

Ms. Shirley was right. I nodded at her in agreement as she continued,

"When I think about true love, I know that it isn't meditated, calculated, and can't be manipulated. It has to be pure, it takes work and more importantly, it requires honesty and commitment."

"Ms. Shirley, I'm committed to my life with Arlington."

"Child, I know you think I'm old and religious, but I want you to know I'm wise. If you don't listen to nothing else that I got to say, listen to me now. Keep your damn mouth shut. Don't contact Arlington at all. When he is ready, he will talk to you. Let him deal with the situation in his own time. If he needs 2 hours, 2 weeks, 2 months or whatever, let him have his time and space. Don't push the envelope. You got it."

"I got it Ms. Shirley, I got it. It's getting late. I better get home so I can be at the hospital first thing in the morning."

"You had me so wrapped up in your mess I forgot to ask how are my babies?"

"They are good. Ariah went home with my parents and AJ just got a broken leg so he will be home in a couple days."

"Alright, I will keep you posted."

Ms. Shirley walked me to the door and watched me pull out of her drive away before closing the door behind me. I was nervous about going home. Ok the truth is I was nervous about being home with Arlington at home. I was concerned that he hadn't called me, his parents, and nobody to tell them what happened.

Arriving at the house, I took a deep breath before hitting the garage door opener. When I didn't see Arlington's truck, I exhaled in relief. The house seemed to possess an eerie stillness to it. I have been home by myself before, but tonight I felt alone. I think I will follow Ms. Shirley's advice and not call Arlington, at least not tonight anyway. It was too late to call my girls to come over so, I guess I will have a bath, a glass of wine and go to bed before I drive myself crazy thinking about everything that happened today.

Early the next morning, I was awakened to the sun shining on my face. I could not believe it was morning already. The funny thing was, I didn't even remember falling asleep. I felt like I had just laid down. It was a little before 8am and I had not heard hair nor hide from Arlington. I promise if he is somewhere all caked up with Piper there is gonna be trouble.

I needed to make sure that everything at the office was situated before I headed up to the hospital to sit with AJ. Just as I thought everything was running like clockwork. After updating the staff on AJ's condition and my schedule, I sat at my desk to return a few calls and emails. Just as I was about to dial out, my mobile phone rang. Cassie's name flashed across the caller id.

"Hey Lady, how is my knucklehead godson doing?"

"You know it would probably take a Mack truck to stop him, with his bad ass."
"He's just like his daddy; would you expect anything different from him?"

Hearing Cassie say, his daddy felt like a dagger pressed against my throat. It sounded like she said that, just to be funny. I'm being paranoid. I got to pull myself together. I know she don't know what's going on, and I ain't about to tell her just yet.

"I just got off the phone with Myra. We are meeting for lunch, before we head up to the hospital for a minute."

"Ok, so I'm not invited. Is it because I'm married? Do my breath stink or what?"

"Yeah, it's early so your breath might be a little tart but that's not why we didn't invite you. We just assumed that you were busy." Cassie said with a chuckle.

"Just so you know, my breath don't stink. But I guess I can grace ya'll with my presence."

"Oh, we are so not worthy. See you at Lenora's at 1."

"I'm heading to the hospital now, so I will holla at cha then."

After hanging up with Cassie, I shut my computer down and left the office for the day. You would have thought that I was being stalked or hunted by the police. I walked into the hospital looking over my shoulder each step of the way. I still was not quite sure what to expect. The quiet storms are always the most deadly. Well I guess I should look on the bright side, if Arlington decided to strangle me at least I am already at the hospital. I made it to AJ's room on the pediatric ward with no issues.

"Hey momma's baby."

"I'm not a baby anymore; remember daddy said I'm his little man."

There go that dagger feeling again. Let me shake that off, for real this time. It's not like I intentionally set out to defraud him, I really thought that he was my son's father. I leaned down to kiss AJ on his forehead.

"No matter how old you get or tall you become you will always be momma's baby."

"Ok, I guess. Where's dad?"

"He's at work but he will be here soon. You can call him on his mobile."

"I don't need to call him. Daddy told me that he will always be here for me, so I know he will be here soon."

"Exactly! You make sure you always believe that too."

The nurse came in to check AJ's vital signs. I need to know if Arlington at least called and checked on his son. I needed to see what the nurse knew.

"Excuse me, but has anyone called looking for me or my husband?"

Flipping through AJ's chart, she responded.

"I just came on duty 2 hours ago and to my knowledge no one has called or come by since you left last night. I can confirm at the nurse's station if you would like me too.

"No thank you. That will not be necessary."

I spent the next couple hours with AJ. Lunch time couldn't have come quick enough. Damn these cartoons. I had endured more than my fair share of digital, loud, high pitched giggling and crashes. I remember the days when cartoons were fun, educational, and without all the damn sound effects.

"Momma will be back. I'm about to go see Tee Tee Cassie and Auntie Myra, then we all will be back up here. I promise I will bring you a special treat."

"Ok, momma I love you. Oh, call daddy and ask him what I want for my special treat. He knows what guys like."

"You're my son and I know what you like too."

"See you in a couple hours son." I made sure I let the nurse's station know to call me if they needed anything, and to make sure they knew I would be right back. I didn't want them to think that we just left our son there alone.

I left the hospital and raced over to Lenora's. This is where me and my girls met for the meeting of the minds during our workday. We've made so many decisions, shed so many tears, and laughed until our faces hurt at this place. Boy if these walls could talk. Both Cassie and Myra were there when I arrived. I needed to put on my game face and pretend like nothing was wrong.

"A party ain't a party til I run through it. Heeey!"

"Alicia, this isn't a party. Sit your behind down."

"Myra, I promise if you get laid, you will be a hell of a lot friendlier. You're wound so tight, when you do cut loose, you are gonna spin outta control."

"My body is a temple, not a do drop in. Thank you."

"Alicia, look at Myra, her got a lil spunk in her trunk today. What's his name?"

"Whose name?"

"The name of the man that has finally took your attention away from Braxton."

"Why it gotta be a man? I am whole, holy, and healthy. This is Jesus joy."

"I know the joy of the Lord is your strength. Even though I said it for you, this does count as one of your scriptures. You only get 2 more scriptures during lunch. And, do tell before I call Pasa and ask him to discern what is going on."

"You could have at least took your purse off your shoulder before you put on your clown suit. If you just gotta know noisy, I have been casually seeing a man. Not as a date, but strictly as friends."

"Alicia you got Ms. Thang to come from behind the veil. Do I need to order a drink in the middle of the day to listen to this story?"

"If ya'll don't stop teasing me, I won't tell you anything."

"Ok we are listening intently."

"The truth is there is nothing to tell. I was at the Bible bookstore and this guy named Darryl introduced himself to me. He was good looking and seemed to be successful. Well, the meat of the matter is, he owns some kind of home design architecture, remodeling business of some sort. He came over personally and fixed a couple things around the house. I finally got the granite counter tops put in my kitchen. He only let me pay for materials, so I cooked a few meals for him. Ray is kind, thoughtful, funny and very respectful."

"I'm sure I speak for Alicia when I say this. But it sounds like Prince Charming caulked, sawed, and hammered his way into your heart."

"I thought so too. But he has a child, and he don't attend church regularly."

"And?"

"And that's enough. I know that my husband is going to be a Bishop, or a Pastor at the very least and his daughter lives with him. He don't want a wife, he wants a nanny."

Cassie and I looked back and forth at each other for a moment. I could not understand she had a perfectly good man but in the fault finding mission all she could find, is the fact that he don't attend church regularly.

"Cassie let me take this one. Everybody walking the face of this earth including Braxton has told you that he is never going to be with you. Let it go and let that man love you the way you love Braxton."

"It was prophesied over me that Braxton was my husband. So until God himself comes down from heaven above and tell me differently, I am standing on His promise."

"God didn't tell you that, Mother whatever her name was told you that almost 15 years ago. He is married, happily married with children. I'm telling you, let that dream go."

"I have faith that God will work it out."

"Ok, keep telling yourself that. I'm still trying to understand you; don't you supposed to be making disciples of men, instead of looking for them?"

"How can two walk together if they don't agree? I can't be yoked up with just anybody."

"Why was he in the bible bookstore, if he don't know the Lord?"

"He was there shopping for a gift for his mother. But I told him not to call me anymore because he was just a distraction."

"I beg to differ. I would say he is the real thing, you are the one that's distracted."

"You have been back with your husband for 10 minutes, now all of a sudden you have turned into a marriage counselor."

"Oh no, I am far from that. Hell a blind man can see the mistake that Myra is making a mile away."

"Ok, I will give you that one."

This conversation was a little heavy for lunch, but we haven't seen each other in a while so we were playing catch up. It was amazing that we managed to actually cram food in our mouths, in between the words that were coming out. I was trying to stay engaged so I wouldn't start thinking about Arlington and the mess I had going on in my life.

"What's going on with Ms. Cassie while you over there cosigning with Alicia?"

"Well, since you brought it up, check out my big girl prize."

Cassie held up her right hand and on it was the biggest diamond that I ever saw in my life. Myra and I just stared in shock.

"Ok are we supposed to say congratulations, I'm sorry, or what? What the hell? You done went out and bought yourself an engagement ring?"

"Hell naw! You know I'm independent, but not that independent. It's against momma's religion to buy myself any left hand jewelry."

"I'm engaged to be married. DJ and I are getting married."

"DJ who? Are we talking about DJ, DJ?

Thee one and only Donovan Jacobson, you actually agreed to become Mrs. Donovan *I'm all that* Jacobson? The world must be coming to an end."

"Well, see what had happened was."

I knew whatever Cassie was about to tell us was a lie because she started her sentence with, what had happened. Lord have mercy she done let this man get her all sprung and thangs.

"Ok, Cassie what had happened was, he hit it right, right, in all the places?"

"No, that ain't it. For the record, if it got any better than what he has already given me then let me tell you I don't want it."

"Please spare us the details, hello saved woman present." Myra said waving her hand at Cassie.

"Myra, let her tell her story, how she has fallen for the most commitment phobic man driving through the streets of Denver."

"Alicia, remember awhile back when I told you he and I started dating again?"

"Yeah, but I know what ya'll call dating." I said with a smirk.

"It wasn't even like that. I don't know what got into DJ. He has actually been courting me. Instead of meeting for happy hour then a coin toss to either go to my house or his, we've been dating. I'm talking about dinners, movies, museums, and visits to his parent's house. And to top it all off, I've been going to church with him. He introduced me to his Pastor."

I know I should be happy for Cassie, but I know this was just a trick and I hate that my girl is actually being so gullible. He is just marinating her to roast her. I got to keep her from making the biggest mistake of her life.

"Cassie you know good and hell well that DJ is not the marrying type. He's married to the streets, the club is his girlfriend and he prides himself on being a hit and run brotha. You know everyone told me that Arlington was no good and you see what I go through. I'm trying to save you some pain and agony."

"It's not even like that. DJ genuinely loves me and he has committed to making me that happiest woman on earth for the rest of my life. He hasn't been to the club in months, he changed his mobile phone number, and are ya'll ready for this? I have a key to his place."

"I am so happy for you Cassie. I went to a seminar that said a woman falls in love then decides to get married and men decide to get married then fall in love. See the Bible says if you delight yourself in the Lord, He will give you the desires of your heart. You've always said there wasn't anything that you didn't like about DJ except he ran the streets like a pair of panty hose. So tell us the details, I better be a bride's maid and don't be tryin to put me in a damn sea foam green, taffeta dress, puffy sleeves and a huge bow on the bootie."

I couldn't believe Myra was egging Cassie on like this. Even if a zebra could change its stripes, it's still a zebra. I needed to keep my girl from making the biggest mistake of her life.

"Listen to me. Cassie you a strong, independent, black woman, doing your own thing with your own money, keep doing you. DJ is just gonna knock you up, leaving you at home to take care of his house and kids while he resumes running the streets. How many kids he got? About 4 kids by 5 different baby mommas? You are the forbidden fruit, the only woman that hasn't fallen for his game. So he had to step his game up. That ring isn't nothing more than a prop to get hooked. Once he does, he will just string you along. You see what I been going through with Arlington these past few months. Girl, don't fall for it."

"Alicia shut your hatin' ass up."

"Oh Ms. Holier Than Thou is cussin' now."

"I already told your ass, hell, and damn are in the Bible so I can say them. But, as I was saying, Cassie you love DJ and ya'll are good together.

Things have worked themselves out. Let that man be a man and become the head of your life, you need to be covered. And, Alicia the whole Arlington thing was your fault. You trusted a stranger over your husband and almost lost a good man, a loving man, a committed man. The only reason that you don't want Cassie to get married is because you feel that you got one up on us because you are the only one of us that is married. Stop hatin' and mind your own self business."

"I don't know Myra maybe Alicia is right." Before Cassie could finish her sentence, Myra interrupted again.

"DJ took you to his church, introduced you to his Pastor, parents, friends, and colleagues, he gave you a ring, and a key. This man has spent time and money showering you continuous attention, adoring, and affection. What more can he do? Lord knows the pool of good, successful, and available men is scarce so you better hold on to DJ. The Bible says he that finds a wife, finds a good thing and obtains favor with the Lord. You were in a position to be found and he found you. Now all you have to do is be a wifey. I am so happy for you."

"You know Myra you are right. I love DJ and I want to be with him so I'm gonna go for what I know. By the way, even though you are on my side, you've met your scripture quota for the day. No mo' words from the Lord for you."

I couldn't believe that the one time we needed Myra to discern what was going on, she let her emotions get the best of her. She is actually cosigning this monstrosity.

"Ok, don't say I didn't tell you so when you call me from your honeymoon to tell me that you caught DJ in bed with the maid." I said as I looked down at my phone, I didn't have any missed calls.

"Myra is right. Quit hatin' and be happy for your girl. Is everything ok? Do we need to go to the hospital now?"

"No, everything is good, why?"

"I noticed that you checked your phone a few times since we've been sitting here."

"AJ just has a broken leg, he's ok. The restaurant is a little loud, so I was just making sure my phone was on vibrate just in case Arlington or the hospital called."

I wasn't gonna tell my girls what was going on with me Arlington especially until I knew what was going on myself. But it did concern me that it has been almost 24 hours since he left the hospital, and I still hadn't heard from Arlington. I understand that he is mad at me, but this here is no reason for him to abandon his kids like this.

I loved spending time with my girls. No matter what was going on we always worked our way through the situation no matter how many martinis and appetizers it took. The sista friend time we spent together was worth the tears and laughter.

After finishing with lunch, the three of us headed to the hospital together. As I walked into the hospital, I saw I truck that looked like Arlington's. Because of how the vehicle was parked, I could not see the plates. I was nervous inside because I didn't know what to expect. Would he go off on me in front of my friends? Will he just give me the cold shoulder, leaving me to explain to the ladies what was going on with us? A feeling of relief calmed me when I saw AJ's room was absent of Arlington's presence.

The ladies and I visited with AJ for a couple hours. By the time he gets this cast off his leg, he's going to be spoiled. He has been showered with gifts, attention, and treats. If I didn't know any better, you couldn't convince me that he was in an accident just yesterday. He was doing everything running around. The nurse said, he hasn't needed any pain meds all day. It was getting late and mom has had Ariah since yesterday. I needed to go pick her up.

"Ya'll can hang out but, I have to go pick up Ariah from my mother's house. Son, I will see you tomorrow. I think you get to come home. YAY!!"

"Well we might as well get outta here too."

"AJ your Tee Tee loves you." Myra and Cassie both kissed AJ on the forehead, before I leaned in to kiss him.

"Son, do you need anything before I leave?"

"No mommy, I'm good. I'm just gonna wait for daddy to come before I go to sleep."

AJ was looking forward to seeing his father. I pray that Arlington wouldn't disappoint him. No matter what the test says, he is still AJ's father.

"Your daddy should be here any minute. I love you son."

"Love you too, see you tomorrow."

Myra, Cassie and I left the room. No sooner than we were an earshot away from the room Myra asked,

"Where is Arlington? He don't love nobody like he loves that little boy. I'm surprised he hasn't made them bring him up a bed so he can stay with AJ."

"Oh, he is pressed for a deadline, so we're taking shifts."

They bought it, they didn't need to know my business just yet. I rode down the elevator in silence as Myra and Cassie chatted. I was in such a zone, I didn't realize that we had reached the main floor and the elevator doors had opened. Until Cassie asked,

"Did you forget something?"

"No, why?"

"When the doors open that means it's time to go, so bring your ass."

"Boy you are so bossy. Ok ladies, thanks for hanging out with me and AJ."

"We are your girls where else would we be. I gotta go and check in with my fiancé now."

"Whatever, I guess I am happy though. Take your time with a long engagement; you know the devil ain't got no patience."

"I'm gonna pretend I didn't hear that and hug your neck anyway. I'll holla at you tomorrow."

I waved my girls goodbye and headed to my mom's to pick up Ariah. I had so many thoughts racing through my head. I know that I am the best thing that ever happened to Arlington so I know he won't just walk away. But, I wondered how he was planning to make me pay for my mistake. As far as I was concerned it was too late to redo the past. We are a family and we will always be a family.

I finally made it to my parent's house. Ariah was sitting on the floor in the family room watching a movie while my mother read her book.

"Hey mom."

"Hey lady, how is AJ doing today."

"He's doing good, getting spoiled to death. He should be coming home tomorrow."

"Girl, count your blessing the situation could have been a lot worse."

"I know. Where's dad? In the garage fiddling around with something, I don't mess with him when he is out there doing his man thang."

I was scared to open a conversation with my mom, but I had to at least get enough information to prove Ms. Shirley wrong about my momma's wisdom when it came to men.

"Momma, daddy has taken you through so many changes why do you stay with him? Do you feel that you are too weak to make it on your own? Is your self-esteem so low that you don't realize you deserve better?"

"Oh honey, I thought I taught you better than that. A woman's strength isn't based on if she can stand alone, it is based on her ability to fight for love."

"But why is it a woman's job to fight, I thought a man is supposed to be a protector and provider."

"That is correct, but a woman is a nurturer. When I met your father, he was a mechanic, happily working on cars. He used to have junk cars parked in the garage, driveway and in front of the house. Rather than whining and complaining, I convinced him to open his own shop. I pulled the money from my 401(k) so he didn't have no excuse for not doing it."

I should have talked to my mom all along about Arlington, it seems that she has a better understanding than I thought she would. She made my dad into something when he wasn't nothing.

"See mom, if it wasn't for me Arlington wouldn't be anything. And, I tell him all the time so he doesn't forget it."

"You are wrong, dead wrong. No baby you didn't let me finish. Your dad was something before I met him, I motivated him to become who he desired to be and the man that I needed him to be. Not once have I reminded him of what I did for him, but I remind him what I am to him."

I couldn't believe that my mother was actually sharing this information with me. She stepped real close to me before she continued,

"Yes, it hurt like hell when I found that your dad had a lady on the side. But, after 25 years of marriage, money, pain, and tears, I was not gonna let him go without a fight. I had too much invested in him to let my marriage go without a fight. Honey, men have selective listening. You can show them better than you can tell them. But more important than the investment, I love my husband enough to fight for our marriage."

My mother placed her hand on mine.

"I don't know what's been going on between you and Arlington but whatever it is; you have to decide if it is worth fighting for."

I just nodded my head. I know my mother was trying to get me to tell her all the drama that I have been going through with Arlington for damn near a year now. All she would do is lecture me and I didn't feel like hearing her mouth. I get enough of that from Ms. Shirley.

"Ok, mom I will remember that."

"You know I'm here if you wanna talk."

"Thanks. Come on Ariah time to go home."

"I guess you know what you're doing. I'll probably see you at the hospital tomorrow. Your dad and I are going camping this weekend, so we will check on that knot head boy before we leave."

"Bye mom."

As I put Ariah in the truck, all I could think about is why everybody seemed to have advice for me about my life. I am a grown ass woman and I was doing just fine making things happen. Just like my momma just told me, whenever Arlington decides to call, I will just have to tell him who the hell he's dealing with. A far as I knew, Arlington was AJ's father so there wasn't anything to tell him.

Usually, Ariah nods off to sleep as we are driving home. But this time, she was wide awake, humming a song and playing with her toys.

"What are you doing back there Ariah?"

"I learned a new song at school today and I'm practicing it for daddy."

I needed to think up a story for Ariah because she is expecting her daddy to be home when we get there. I was willing to bet my bottom dollar that Arlington was not going to be there.

"Ariah let me hear your song; daddy is going to stay with AJ tonight so he won't be home when we get there."

"Ok, I'm gonna wait for daddy, he likes me to sing."

"I like you to sing too?"

"I'll just save it for him until he comes home."

I watched Ariah in the rearview mirror. It seemed like soon as I told her that her daddy wasn't going to be home she went off to sleep. I swear this little girl had Arlington by the heart strings. I know beyond a shadow of a doubt that Ariah was Arlington's child so as long as I had at least one of his kids, I can be certain that he won't stray too far.

I arrived home. Arlington's truck was not in the garage but, it looked like he had been home. I noticed that the suit he wore yesterday was the in dry cleaning basket. I got me and Ariah ready for bed. The next move was on. We'll just have to see what tomorrow brings.

All The King's Men

I stormed out of the hospital after hearing that AJ wasn't my son. I was so hurt that I had left the hospital before seeing that my son was alright. I was choked up and couldn't speak. I couldn't believe that Alicia would hate me so much to hurt me like this. I didn't deserve this. AJ is my seed, my solider. He was the reason that I gave so much of myself to my marriage. It was my responsibility to see that my son becomes a man by seeing a man rather than trying to imitate a reflection of masculinity.

I had visions of him being All American, getting recruited for college, being drafted into the pros. My son's acceptance speech was not going to be the cliché love God and thank you momma. A shout out was going to go out to me, his father too. I was supposed to be a vital part of my son's success. I never thought that I would have a baby momma without a baby. Alicia has always said Arlington, I made you. She is right; she made me love a kid that wasn't mine and she made me marry a woman I didn't love.

I sat in my truck inside the parking garage at the hospital and cried. The pain of knowing my son was not my son, hit me like a ton of bricks. All I could do is cry like a baby. Every time I heard a car door slam, it felt like another stab in my heart. I know a grown man ain't supposed to cry but, damn it, I love my son!

After the tears finally dried up, I started my car and began to drive aimlessly. I had no idea where I was going, but I couldn't stop driving. Memories of my son kept flashing through my mind like movie clips. I remember the first time I held him, the first time he said daddy. I have been here for all of his firsts, but it looks like I will miss what is to come.

After driving all night, I pulled up to my house. I saw that Alicia's truck wasn't in the garage. That was a sigh of relief. There was no way I could face her right now. I needed to get cleaned up and pack a bag so I don't have to come home for a few days.

As I walked upstairs, I passed AJ's room; tears began to swell in my eyes. I shut his bedroom door and headed straight to the shower, praying that Alicia would not catch me here. I needed to get myself together before I faced her, AJ, or anyone for that fact of the matter.

I sat on the bed to get dressed, my heart ached. I have never felt hurt like this. But I had to move past this moment and decide what it is that I needed to do. I needed to tell somebody, anybody what was going on. I decided to go holla at my father. He was a recovered playa and wise as hell. I was too embarrassed to tell anybody else that I had gotten caught up.

I made it to my father's house and let myself in. If you didn't have your own key or if the back door wasn't open, chances were you wasn't gonna get in. My father would not get up and answer the door for nobody. Once my father went into the basement, anything short of a fire and an act of congress wasn't getting him back upstairs that day, and sometimes days on end.

My parents divorced years ago and rather than getting a new wife, he created a new life by turning the house into the ultimate bachelor pad. The main level of the house had the usual; you know living, dining room, kitchen, two bedrooms and two bathrooms. But downstairs, downstairs was what my father referred to as his piece of heaven on earth. He completely transformed his walk out basement into a luxury man cave. There was a fully stocked wet bar, state of the art audio/visual center, and a master suite, complete with a Jacuzzi tub.

As you could imagine more often than not there wasn't a reason for him to go upstairs because right outside the sliding glass doors was the granddaddy of grills. I think that grill could do everything but hunt for dinner. I came down stairs and just as I thought, my father was sitting in his recliner watching the game. I took off my jacket and sat on the couch.

"Pops, you won't believe what I am about to tell you. AJ ain't my son."

"What that boy do now? He probably did something you did when you was his age. He must be feeling better now, if he's getting on your nerves to the point that you've disowned him. Is he running the nurses at the hospital crazy?"

"No dad, I ain't AJ's father!"

"Son, you can't disown the kids because you are mad at Alicia either? What the hell did that girl do now?"

"You should be asking who she did. Pops, I am not AJ's biological father."

I said with a sigh as I sat on the sofa.

"What the hell! Son, what are you talking about?"

"Man, dad trip this. Alicia and I were at the hospital with AJ yesterday. You know, I called you after we knew he was out the woods. Well, the doctor mentioned AJ might need a transfusion. I thought the transfusion should come from one of his people, that way we know the blood is good. Both Alicia and I went to the lab and gave blood. Turns out everything was all good and he didn't need the blood. Long story short the doctor said his blood type didn't match me or Alicia, so it was impossible for AJ to be my son."

"Shut the hell up? What did Alicia say?"

"Not a damn thing. What could she say? She stood there looking surprised, surprised that she was busted. I didn't know I wasn't AJ's father and apparently Alicia wasn't planning on me ever finding out."

"Arlington for real, you got to be shitting me."
"I didn't give her a chance to say anything. I punched the wall and walked out. I drove around all night, stopped at the house to get cleaned up and then I came here."

"Has she at least tried to explain the situation?"

"Nope, an *I'm sorry* or *let me explain* won't help her this time. She hasn't had the gall to call, email, or text me. What excuse do you think she could give for lying to me every day for the past six years?"

"How the hell did you get mixed up with this girl? I know ya'll wasn't together when she got pregnant. You didn't go get a blood test did you?

Wait before you answer that let me get you a drank. I know you don't drink no more but, this is definitely a shot, not a beer moment."

My father got up to pour us a shot of Martell in a couple of brandy snifters. Pops hit the mute button on the remote control to silence the game before sitting back down.

"Ok son, go ahead tell me how you let yourself get caught up like this? That boy looks just like you though, but you know they say feed a kid long enough they'll start looking like you."

"Well, you know she showed up on mom's doorstep with the baby and was like this is Arlington's son. So mom let her in. She thought AJ looked like me for no other reason than he had dark skin and light eyes like I do. Mom was convinced and said that it was my baby. And you know how momma is, once she thinks she knows something, it becomes fact."

My dad sat up in his recliner and just looked at me for a minute before he said,

"Boy I should bust you in your mouth for saying some ignorant shit like that. You know good and hell well that you should have went and got a blood test before you even knew that baby's name. And, your momma wanted grandkids so bad, the boy could have come out with red hair and blue eyes and she would have said the baby was yours. But that still doesn't explain why you married her."

As embarrassed as I was to tell anybody the truth, I knew I had to be 100 with pops and if anybody could help get me out this hell he could.

"Man, this is what happened. I met Alicia at the watering hole. I was there kicking it with the fellas. You know how it goes, we in there just bullshitting, talking about the game, paying debts with shots. Alicia was always posted in there. She looked good as hell, she was always fly hair done, make-up straight, pushing a clean 300, and from what I saw none of the fools up in there had ever hollered at her. I was a little hesitant to get at her at first because she always had her ass or tits on display, leaving nothing to the imagination, she was out as much as I was, and she cussed like a sailor. Alicia had more cuss words than breaths coming out her mouth."

"Son, I've told you time and time again always follow your first mind, you should have swatted and left that bar fly by her damn self. There was a reason she was there and nobody else had got with her. But you thought you should show everybody that you were the Mack."

"I know, she was fine and all but, I just wanted to hit, and I knew she wouldn't object. We talked a little but nothing big you know she was just a fixture until… Man I got drunk as hell one night and she offered to take me home needless to say that I never made it. You know I tapped that, with no intentions of ever getting with her again. You know how that goes, she became convenient. I never had to take her out, introduce her to nobody, or even spend the night. I decided to holla at her a couple times on the phone, but her conversation didn't interest or stimulate me. But I chilled with her for a minute you know hollering at her on the phone every now and then. She was getting all attached, I told her we were gonna have to chill because I wasn't feeling her like that. Two weeks later almost to the date, she called and said she was pregnant."

"For real Arlington, you were slippin' on your pimpin'. That was a set up; you should have saw that one coming a mile away. You know better than to run raw with a jump off. Boy, I know I taught you better than that. How did she move from jump off to wifey?"

I swallowed my drink in a single gulp and began to pour me another shot. Pops repeated himself.

"I need to know how she moved from jump off to wifey? She was on the fast track."

"Once again, I had a Yak attack; you know I had been throwing 'em back for a minute. I was too drunk to drive home. I called and asked if I could crash at her spot for the night, you know I could damn near walk to her place from the spot. I laid in bed by myself. It was so late that I didn't even look in on AJ before shutting it down. I rolled over in the middle of the night and you know what happened next."

My father shook his head in disappointment and said,

"Damn, you hit it again, didn't you?"

"Yep, I slept in it. Then to make matters worse, I got some on my way out the door. You know how that goes. I woke up and rolled right into before I knew it I was busting one. Get this though, I knew I had messed up the second I started cumming. I tried to pull out, but it was too late. You know the rest. I had two kids by the broad, so I had to man up and marry her instead of just breaking her off all my loot and having her barking in my ear about my kids and my business. Hell, this is the first drink I had since she told me she was pregnant the second time. I realized I do some stupid shit when I'm drunk."

"Well, I gotta ask is Ariah your daughter?"

"At this point your guess is good as mine but, you know I'm gonna go get that checked. What I can't understand is that she has been throwing this whole trust issue thing at me about Piper and all along she's been holding this lie so close to her heart, she believed it was the truth."

Pop's voice was reduced to a subtle murmur. He raised his eyebrow, shook his head and ran his fingers across his chin before he began to speak.

"Arlington, damn I ain't got nothing for you man. I don't what the hell you should do."

"I got a bag in the truck to last me for a few days. I'll probably post up here for a few days until I figure something out."

"You know you welcome, but at some point you are gonna have to go to the hospital to check on AJ. Even though he is not your son, you are still that boy's daddy."

"I know. I just gotta go when Alicia ain't there because I will probably choke her out if I see her right now. Woman or no woman, she will catch a beat down right about now. Dad, I have been up all night, I'm going upstairs to crash for a minute."

I headed upstairs with hopes that my mind would quit racing long enough for me to at least close my eyes for a couple of minutes. For the first time in my life, I can say I felt heartache. It seemed like I had just closed my eyes when I woke up to my phone vibrating. Before grabbing my phone, I glanced at the clock only to discover that I had been sleep for more than five hours. I grabbed my phone to see that I had a few missed calls and texts from my boy Eric. I wasn't expecting a call from Alicia but I was surprised that she hadn't called using AJ's condition as an excuse to call. I decided to holla back at Eric.

"What's up E?"

"I can't call it. How's the boy?"

"He alright, you know that boy too hardheaded to have any serious damage."

"I hear ya. Where you at?"

"I'm over here at pop's crib, swing through I need to holla at cha."

"Fo, sho. I'm in route."

I needed to let go of this mess. I went back downstairs.

"Boy, I was on my way up there, I thought maybe you fell into a coma or something."

"Naw, I'm good. I been up for a minute. I holla'd at the fool E before I came down."

"What's up with him?"

"Chillin, he's about to slide through."

"Ok, you good."

"I'm straight."

I looked up to see Eric coming through the patio door.

"How's it going my people?"

"Man, its slow motion 'round here. You might as well grab a shot before you sit down."

"Oh don't tell me the Cavs are losing? They were up by ten when I left the crib."

"Man, they got it, Lebron got his clown suit on. Wait til you see the highlights. His shots are just nasty. I got to tell you about this hoe shit Alicia done pulled."

"Oh hell, don't tell me it's your fault that AJ got hit by the car, even though you were at work and he was with her."

"Trip this, I was at the hospital yesterday and found out that AJ ain't mine."

"Ain't your what?"

"Ain't my seed."

"Fool, how much have you had to drink before I got here? That boy got a peanut head just like you and he acts just like your stupid ass. Get the hell outta here."

My dad looked at Eric with the no-nonsense look and nodded his head up and down. Eric looked at me and back at my dad.

"For real?"

Both my pops and I nodded continuously as he looked back and forth at us again.

"You damn right, I need a drink."

After Eric poured his shot, he sat the bottle on the bar and looked up at us again.

"For real. Damn what the hell do the slut got to say for herself? No disrespect."

"That slut, like you said ain't got a damn thing to say. Hell, what can she say other than God is the daddy?"

"Man, what the hell. I don't even know what to say."

"I can't believe I married that hoe. What was she doing sneaking a fool in the back door as I was leaving out the front door? How nasty can a bitch be? She just letting everybody run raw."

"Did she at least tell you who she thinks her baby daddy is?"

"I bet her nasty ass don't know her damn self. What's funny is I knew when she told me that she was pregnant that baby wasn't mine. That is why ya'll didn't know I was expecting until the baby got here."

"Arlington I know you are pissed off and you have the right to be but, she is still the mother of at least one of your kids so try to be respectful."

"Pops, how can I respect somebody that would lie to me, betray me, and play me like that? I don't think of her as a lady no more, she is just a nasty ass hoe to me. To tell you the truth I want to find her and punch her in the mouth. She want to hoe like a dude, I sure in the hell can treat her like one."

"Son, I know you are pissed and you have every right to be. Do you know why I taught you how to play chess?"

"Yeah, to punish me and keep me off the streets." Pops let out a light chuckle then said.

"I taught you how to play chess to teach you how to think and respond to your opponents in life. You can be an attacker or a quiet positional player. No matter what you choose, have a game plan a strategy. In chess we use a term call swindle, it is when a player is in a losing position and converts his position into a win or draw. You know what I'm saying?"

"Pops come on. Chess?"

"Since you ain't feeling chess, I'm gonna let that marinade for a minute and bring it to you a different way. Check out Lebron. He plays like he got home court advantage no matter whose court it is. He makes people play to his standards, he don't respond to theirs. You are a man, set the order you decide what happens next. Are you gonna leave, stay, welcome another man into your son's life, what?"

"Arlington man, Pops is right. Are you prepared to go home to your son playing ball in the front yard with your wife's baby daddy? Brotha man gonna be at the games, showing up on holidays, at yo crib making sammiches, drinking beer, talking about we cool."

"The hell with that! I don't know what's gonna happen, but I know for damn sure I ain't about to have nobody's baby daddy at my crib. I'm mad you would even think I would play myself like that."

"I'm just saying. You let that bitch call the shots and you will be a guest in your house that you pay for. While she is walking around like ain't nothing wrong. Before long she'll have you fools dressed alike, with a daddy chore calendar for ya'll to follow. Her girls will be egging her on telling her, *she's the biggest boss that you seen thus far* and singing one of this man hating independent theme songs."

"How much have you drank, because you got me fucked up. I don't know nothing about the weak ass brothas she used to dealing with but, I'm a grown ass man and I refuse to let a hoe steal my manhood."

We couldn't help but laugh about the situation. I finally get what people mean when they say life is funny. This mess that Alicia has pulled is so outlandish that it is funny. Nobody in their right mind could ever think up something this crazy.

"It's too late to throw something on the grill, let's order some wings or something. It looks like we will be here chilling for a minute."

"Eric you forgot we at Pop's house it's never too late to fire up the grill. He keeps Brats and Link on standby just for occasions like this."

"Tell him son, you know how I do. Let me get the party started."

My dad got up to get the food going. Eric and I sipped on our beers watching the game. The room was too quiet. I know Eric was trying to find something to say to help his boy, and I was trying not to think of all the ways I could kill Alicia and get away with it.

"I ain't trying to jump the gun or anything, but you 'bout single now. We can go check a couple traps. You bound to run into a jump off. A good ride will do the body good."

"Good looking out, but I'm straight. Hell a jump off is what got me in this situation in the first place."

"Man, whatever happened to what's her name? That fine ass chocolate dime you was about to marry, you know who I'm talking about."

"You talking about Avery."

"Yep, Avery. What's up with that?"

"Thanks to Alicia ain't nothing up with that.

Avery is married and living in DC, Virginia or somewhere that way."

"That girl loved yo dirty drawls. How'd you let somebody else snatch her up?"

"I've done a lot of stuff that I ain't proud of, but screwing Alicia and losing Avery is the only thing I regret."

"Like that?"

"Yeah man. Me and Avery was talking about getting married and shit. I loved her for real but she was a good girl. You know into the church, didn't drink, wasn't breaking off none of that. But one thing for damn sure is I know she had my back. Quiet as it's kept I think I would rather have her by my side than you, if I was in a fight."

"Fuck you, that's why she ain't here with your ignorant ass now."

"Well, you know what was up with Alicia, you were there when we hooked up and stuff. Well, I was only gonna hit and quit that, so when she told me she was pregnant I said it wasn't mine because you know her name was in a couple fools mouths. Because I never thought the baby was mine, I never told anybody that she was pregnant. Well you know after Alicia showed up at mom's, got her on her side, I had to come clean. Even though I cheated on Avery, I knew she was my true love and the one I wanted to spend my life with, but I needed to get some stuff out my system before I settled down. When I told her that Alicia had my baby she said ok and was out."

"If she was out just like that, you didn't need her no way. You need a ride or die girl."

"I wish you were right. Avery didn't leave me because I cheated or because of the baby. She left because I didn't tell her. She said that I didn't protect her. You know how punk ass niggas are. Somebody felt it was their responsibility to tell Avery about Alicia."

"You mean Avery knew and she didn't say anything? You better be glad she left. She would have held that over your head for the rest of your life."

"Naw man, Avery wasn't like that. That was what made Avery so special. She forgave me when I cheated, lied, was drunk and everything else. She never made me feel bad when my paper wasn't right. She told me a couple things that really hit home and made me really feel like I wasn't worth having her. She actually told me, if I really loved her, I would have protected her from hurting without being there to comfort her and not trusting her enough to handle the truth."

"That is pretty deep."

"I couldn't argue my point after that. I thought I was protecting her by not telling her what was up."

Pops was back in the room as I was talking.

"Listen to me son, you too Eric. You should never let a story beat you home. See when Avery said you didn't protect her she meant, you left her open to any interpretation of the story and allow her to look like a fool. I don't know where you got your player training from because you didn't get it from me. You want to deal the cards and play her hand. You doing too much, when you didn't tell her what was up all that time, she made up stories in her mind about why you didn't tell her. All women do that. They have to know what's going on, or they will go with what's going on in their minds."

"Pops, that's real talk. Arlington you should have handled that out the gate."

"I never told Avery because I believed in my heart that Alicia wasn't pregnant by me. See if I would have told her, then found out the baby wasn't mine, I would have confessed to cheating when I didn't have to."

"Son, wrong thought pattern. You should have spoke up from jump. Hell, you know a jump off can't keep her damn mouth shut. She knew all along that baby wasn't yours, but she put it on who she knew would accept it without a fight."

After the game went off, Eric decided to bounce. This would be my chance to check on AJ. I called the hospital to check on him, the nurse told me that my wife had just left to go change clothes. I knew that gave me at least an hour that I could go see my son.

When I walked into the hospital room, my son's face lit up like a Christmas tree.

"Daddy, look I got a cast on my leg. I can move it and it doesn't hurt either."

I looked at AJ use his hands to lift his leg off the bed. My son was trying to show his dad that he was strong.

"That's my soldier. Before too long you won't have to wear that heavy cast."

"The nurse said tomorrow I can walk with crutches and if I do real good, I can take them home and walk with them until they take the cast off."

"I will help you practice walking on crutches. You will be the best boy to ever walk on crutches."

"Dad, I am sad because the nurse also said I have to wait about two months before I can play football again."

"Don't be sad son, we will just have to play Madden until we can go outside and play together."

"Yeah, I can try out some new plays and stuff from that I learned from Madden when I can walk without crutches."

Looking down at AJ, I have never been so proud of my son. AJ was my dude, and nothing was going to change that. My son was strong just like me. I wouldn't even know how to walk away from the joy that this little boy brought me. Between watching the clock and the visits from the nurses, I just kicked it with my dude. I have always made time for him, but it was something about this moment that was special.

I knew in my heart there was no way that I could or would be a part-time father. I would sacrifice my life so that my son would live. I am a male by nature but a man by choice which made the answer to what I needed to do obvious. I knew time was winding down and I had to get out of the hospital before Alicia showed up. I was still so mad, that I could spit.

"Son, your daddy loves you and I will be back tomorrow."

Looking down at what I wrote on his cast. AJ looked at me with the biggest brightest eyes and said,

"Dad, I have the coolest, best dad ever. I'm gonna be just like you when I grow up."

I gave AJ some dap before I walked out the hospital door. My heart was weeping. It seemed as though as I was walking down the hallway towards the elevator that, the building was crumbling down around me brick by freakin' brick.

I stood in the lobby of the hospital. I needed to figure out where the hell was I about to go. My first thought was to go back to pops but, I know if I go there, I will be drunk for the next few days. I was not trying to turn back to the bottle. I worked too hard to control that and I was not going to let it get the best of me. Going home was not an option either. Alicia was the last person I wanted to see right now.

I drove around for a while and found myself in front of Piper's house. I don't know why I came here. I haven't talked to her in damn near a year. And, the last time we talked, I cussed her out. I knew I should have called but, I don't have her number in my phone anymore. What the hell, I'm here now. I thought. I got out the car and headed to the door.

I rung the doorbell and stepped back off the porch onto the stairs. Piper opened the door once she saw me, she opened the screen door.

"Hey Arlington, this is a pleasant surprise come on in."

"Is it cool, I ain't interrupting anything am I?"

"No you're good. What's up?"

"I'm cool. I just need to sit down for a minute."

The room was tense. I sat on the sofa and she sat in the chair. Neither one of us said anything to the other. I began watching the movie that she had on TV before I got there.

"Arlington, are you hungry?"

"Yeah, I can eat but, don't put yourself out."

"No problem, I got some pork chops that I was gonna cook tomorrow I can fix you a couple with a salad and corn on the cob, is that cool?"

"That's fine Piper, but please don't go through any trouble."

"I'm good, go ahead and get comfortable. I'll be in the kitchen holla at me if you need anything."

"Ok, is it ok if I turn to see what's on?"

"By all means make yourself at home. Don't be acting all brand new."

I flipped through the channels and found a game. It seemed like Piper was only gone 10 minutes and came out with the best looking plate I done seen since the last time I had dinner at my mother's house. Cooking was not one of Alicia's better attributes, but I didn't marry her because she could cook.

"What do you want to drink, water, beer, wine, pop, red kool-aid or milk?"

"Oh you trying to clown on the low. Water is cool."

Me and Piper ate dinner on the coffee table as we watched the game. It was so quiet up in this house that you could hear the sweat from the players hitting the court. But I didn't know what to say, I was stuffed though.

"Thanks Piper, everything was perfect, that really hit the spot. I appreciate it. Can I help you clean up?"

"Naw, I'm good. You know you ain't trying to bust no suds."

"I ain't afraid of no dishwater." I said as I stood up off the sofa.

"Sit down, I got this. I promise." Piper said with a smile as she carried our dishes to the kitchen.

I promise Piper was cool people. My shoes got a little tight, so I took them off. You know that meant the "itis" was kicking in. I took off my shoes and before I knew it I was out like a light.

I heard a loud buzz, and jumped up only to find that it was already morning, and the landscapers were outside doing their thing. I could not believe that I fell asleep and slept so peaceful. While I was sleep, Piper had covered me with a blanket. She was nowhere to be found. I got up and began walking through her house to use the bathroom.

I heard Piper upstairs singing with the song that was playing. Let me just say she was a better cook than singer.

I guess Piper must have heard me flush the toilet and wash my hands. When I walked out the bathroom, Piper was heading down the stairs.

"Good morning sleepy head. You want some breakfast?"

"I'm good, I better get out of here."

I felt like I needed to apologize to her because she didn't have to welcome me into her home, especially after everything I've said and done. As I started to put on my shoes I said,

"Piper, you are cooler than the other side of the pillow and, you know."

"Yeah, I know. And, I'm sorry about everything too. Just know that I'm your friend no matter what and if you need to come sit down, you know that you can over here. No strings attached. You have to find peace somewhere. If you need to talk, just holla at me, we're cool."

I gave Piper a tight hug. She felt good and her house felt right. I couldn't let myself get caught up. Not that Piper wasn't all that but, anything tastes good when you're hungry. But the nice thing about being hungry is you have choices. It's the starving man that has problems he'll eat anything. Right now, the last thing I needed was more woman flavored drama. Piper never brought up the past, it was refreshing to just chill.

I left Piper's house and headed to my dad's to get cleaned up for the day. Wasn't nobody up but me and the sun. I had to get my mind right to deal with Alicia's silly ass. The hospital mentioned that AJ was supposed to be released today. I was looking forward to my son coming home, even though I had no desire to be there. I was surprised that my dad was up when I got home.

"Hey Pops. Why are you up so early?"

"I got it like that. See son, when you retire, your days begin and end when you say so. My question for you is why are you back so late? I know you grown but um, you didn't hook up with a one night stand did you?"

I can't believe Pops was trying to get into my business.

"Look at you all up in mine. Naw, I ended up falling asleep at Piper's."

"Ain't she the gal that got all this mess started in the first place?"

"Well yeah, believe it or not although she hurt me, she had my best interest at heart. She knew Alicia wasn't no good and she was trying to get me away from her at all costs. But you know what dad? She is people. I mean I know no matter what that chick got my back."

"So, what you gon' holla? They always say if you gonna cheat, cheat with somebody you don't mind being with, just in case you get caught."

"It ain't even like that. Me and Piper are just cool, I never thought of her like that."

"Is she a mud duck, chicken head or something?"

"Naw, she straight. Look good, body on point, head on straight, got some change. But she just ain't somebody I want."

Pops chuckled and sat up straight in his recliner and said,

"Son sometimes getting what you need will give you what you want. You didn't need or want Alicia and look what it got you? If you can't think of a reason why not, then I say go for what you know. I'm just saying you need a good woman to help you raise them kids if you divorce Alicia. You know Alicia ain't trying to be a momma."

"Pops, I hear you, Piper is cool, she handles business. But, I'm just not feeling her."

After giving me a sly grin Pops leaned back into his recliner and continued to watch the news. I headed upstairs to get myself together. I couldn't help but shake my head because of Pops. He haven't had a woman on his arm in a minute. What makes him think he still got game? I'm mad he just assumed that I was going to divorce Alicia. At this point, I still don't know what I'm going to do. I do know that I want my family though.

Check

AJ was home from the hospital and Arlington came back home from his father's house. Other than the fact that Arlington made me take both kids in for a blood test, he never mentioned anything about that day in the hospital. The tests confirmed that Ariah was Arlington's only child.

When we got the paperwork, he read the results and handed them to me so that I could read them. After I read the papers, I sat them on the table. I could not say a word and neither did Arlington. I still didn't have an explanation for him.

Something was different about Arlington. With all that we had going on, he was way too calm and peaceful. Things for me were tense. I remembered I put the blood test results on the table, but they weren't there anymore. I was too afraid to ask Arlington did he put them away or what.

Arlington engulfed himself with the kids while avoiding me like the plague. He would read Ariah bedtime stories and "accidently" fall asleep in her bed. Anything that he could do that didn't involve me he did it. Arlington even fell asleep in his man cave watching the game. We were literally two ships that passed in the night. I can't remember the last time he touched me, but in public he put on the persona that we were an ideal, happily married couple. Things were working or shall I say functioning. I wasn't going to press my luck. I'm not gonna dwell on this anymore, I guess I will keep doing me.

Cassie was serious about marrying DJ. I knew she was making a mistake, but this was her little red wagon, she could either push it or pull it. I was not going to stand in her way. She asked that I help her with planning the wedding. Of course, I was honored when she asked to be her matron of honor. She also chose Myra as her maid of honor.

The girls and I met for brunch to work out the details of Cassie's special day. I showed up with my wedding planning book and an empty one for Cassie.

"Alicia I promise you, if you try to start taking over my wedding. I will see that you wear that sea foam green, taffeta dress, with a big bow on your booty." Cassie said with a grin.

"I'm not bossy; I just know what you supposed to be doing." I said before sticking my tongue out at Cassie.

"We are having a simple wedding, with a reception so big, this town won't know what hit it. DJ and I would like to get married at the Meadowlark Country Club it has an excellent view of the mountains. We are only having about 100 guests. Can you manage to help me with this without turning it into a circus?"

"I guess I can do this for you this time. Note to self, cancel the doves and the marching band."

We all laughed. Myra seemed a little distant. I caught Cassie's attention and signaled her that Myra was looking a little sad. Cassie put her hand on Myra's hand and said,

"God has someone great for you. He is just getting him together before he sends him to you. Before you know it, we will be three old married women, at the park feeding our grandkids some ice cream. And, letting them make a huge mess for their momma 'nem to clean up."

"There is no doubt in my mind that God has someone special reserved just for me. I was just thinking how God works in mysterious ways."

"Once and for all, read my lips. Braxton ain't your husband. Quit asking God to change his mind. No means no!"

"Whatever, we are not here to talk about me. We are here to get you over the broom before DJ comes to his senses and tries to throw you back into the sea of single women."

"You and Alicia can kiss my entire ass. I'm getting married. I will kill him dead if he changes his mind. It will be a wedding and funeral at the same time. I would have to marry him, and then kill him so I can collect benefits."

No matter what I'm going through, hanging with my girls was the best way to lift my spirit. They were crazy but, I love them to death. The plans for the wedding were coming together nicely. It was a little frightening though. Anything this easy could not be good. I was so happy for Cassie. After Edmond, I never thought she would love again much less decide to get married. After finalizing the plans, we chatted for few minutes.

"Did knuckle head get his cast off yet? Girl yes, praise the Lord! That is where Arlington is today. AJ was beginning to think he was king of the universe. He has gotten spoiled. We can stop at the gas station without people ooohhing and aaahhhing giving him money, stickers, toys, candy and whatever else they want to send him home with."

"Quit fussing and let AJ have his moment. You know the minute he gets that cast off Arlington is going to have him on some field, court, or somewhere trying to get his star athlete up at it again."

"Don't I know it." I said with a sigh. This is the first me time I have in weeks. I didn't want this day to end, but I had to get home.

"Speaking of which, yeah I gotta go and check in with DJ, to see how his honey do's are coming along."

"Lord, we've created a monster Cassie actually gets to be in charge of somebody."

"Bye ya'll, with ya'll hatin' asses."

I got home to find that the kids and Arlington were gone. I called his mobile phone to see where they were.

"Hey honey, where are you and the kids?"

"We are at the zoo. AJ wanted to celebrate getting his cast off."

"You should have called me, I would have loved to meet ya'll."

"We are ok, do your thing and we'll see you later."

I would have thought that officially knowing that AJ wasn't his son, Arlington would have started playing favorites by now. If anything, it's the opposite. He's loving them both more and spending more time with them than before.

Since I was already out, I decided to run my errands for Cassie's wedding and start planning her shower. We decided not to have a bachelorette party. I ain't mad about it. God only knows that we aren't spring chickens anymore and can't be out partying all night then be picture perfect the next day.

Cassie's big day was finally here. It was wedding day. Everything and everyone was present and accounted for, even Arlington. Me, Arlington, and the kids were all in the wedding. DJ was short one groomsman and it only made sense for Arlington to step in. Damn, my husband was looking good in his tux. Maybe he would get sentimental on me so we can kiss and make up. I miss being bundled in those strong arms. We haven't had sex in months.

The wedding was heavenly, and Cassie looked stunning. I was so happy for her, she deserved a good man. DJ looked like he was entranced in his love for Cassie. I think tears swelled up in his eyes a few times during the ceremony. I remember when Arlington used to look at me like that. I need to become that glimmer in his eye again.

During the reception Arlington and I danced a few times but, I could feel that it was just for show. We wore ourselves out at the reception.

Arlington looked like he was having fun. As long as there is booze and a recent game to talk about, you can keep men entertained for hours. We left the reception early since we had the kids with us. The kids were a snore away from being comatose. Arlington carried both of them to the truck. I loved the fact that I married a big old field hand. If nothing else, I bet I get lucky tonight.

After making it home, Arlington put the kids in bed. I needed to get Arlington's attention; the mood was already right. I timed it just right that when he walked in the room, I was bending over taking off my thigh highs. But I don't think Arlington even looked in my direction.

"Alicia where did you put the bag that the tuxedo came in?" Arlington asked as he walked out the closet. Standing in lingerie, I walked over to him and stood very close to him as I reached behind the door for the bag that was hanging on the back of the door. Arlington didn't even flinch.

"Thanks." He said before walking into the bathroom. Arlington came out of the bathroom dressed for bed. Instead of getting in bed with me, he headed out the bedroom.

"Where are you going?" I asked.

"I'm going to check out Sports Center to see all the highlights."

That was odd since we had a 46 flat screen in our bedroom. I guess this was one of his "accidentally" falling asleep nights.

After I finished getting ready for bed, I went downstairs for a glass of juice. Arlington was standing at the fireplace with the flames flickering. That was odd. It was 80 degrees outside, and the central air was already on. I watched Arlington wipe his face with his hand, turn off the fireplace and lay down on the sofa. I slipped back upstairs before he knew I was watching. The next morning after the kids got on their school bus I confronted Arlington.

"We need to talk." I said.

"I know not now though, I have to go to work."

"We need to deal with our problems. We have ignored them long enough." I said as I grabbed Arlington's arm. He pulled away from me and repeated himself.

"I said, not now."

I let him go ahead out the door. Can't nobody say I didn't try. Arlington called me at the office and invited me to dinner at Jharri's. I was elated, it was our special place. The ambiance was romantic and intimate. Jharri's overlooked the city, complete with a piano bar and VIP lounge.

I didn't know what to expect since Arlington and I hadn't been on a date in months and other than an exchange of essential conversation, we hadn't talked in weeks either. But, I was excited because the last time we went to Jharri's he surprised me with a trip to Jamaica and a new three karat wedding ring. The way he was playing his cards, Arlington was bound to get lucky tonight.

I received Arlington's dinner invitation around noon with reservations for 7PM. That meant I didn't have a lot of time to transform from stunning to dazzling. I needed to leave the office for a quick pampering session and pull out all of Arlington's favorites, everything from his favorite hair style to his favorite perfume. I was prepared to have my whole husband back. I was pulling out all the stops. I even had my assistant go prep the house for the perfect after dinner rendezvous. Myra agreed to pick up the kids for me from school and keep them over night. Everything was perfect.

"It's show time," I thought. It was time for me to put on the best performance of my life. I was going to remind Arlington that he had the best woman walking the face of the earth. I had my game face on, ready to do my thing. I arrived at the restaurant before Arlington but, I sat in the car and watched him walk in. I was too dazzling not to make an appearance. I had to make the entrance as a vision of loveliness and captivate the attention of everyone in the room.

After making my final check in the rearview mirror of my truck, I headed inside the restaurant. The hostess escorted me to the table. I was a splendor of beauty surfacing through the crowd. When I got to the table Arlington's face lit up and his eyes sparkled. He stood up squeezed me tightly and kissed me on the lips.

"Wow Alicia you look magnificent."

"Thank you, after a long day at the office I just kinda through myself together." I wasn't about to let him know that I had went through so much trouble. I was ready to put everything behind us, but I still needed to maintain the upper hand. Arlington wasn't running nothing but his mouth. But, you know I had to make him think he had the situation under control. With all things being equal, all of this could have been avoided if he would have understood that I was the best thing that happened to him, and made a commitment to me before I slept with my ex years ago.

Dinner was great. Jharri's shrimp scampi and lobster tail was too die for. At the suggestion of the waiter, Arlington picked the perfect wine.

Arlington and I engaged in small talk. I could tell he

was leading up to his big moment. I hate to see a grown man grovel, so I won't play too hard to get.

The waiter finally returned for our dessert orders. I was excited because everything was perfect. With dinner coming to an end, Arlington was about to let me know the reason that we met for dinner.

"Alicia, thank you for meeting me tonight. This place holds so many special memories for us. That is why I wanted to come here so we can close this chapter of our life. We have endured more than our fair share of hell over the past year."

I controlled my excitement with a subtle smile and nodding my head in agreement. Arlington sat up straight in his chair. He cleared his throat as he reached across the table, grabbed my hands, and looked straight into my eyes.

"Alicia, we have been through hell over the last year or so. In spite of all the pain and disappointments, I can truly say it was worth it."

"I'm sorry for causing you so much pain. But anything worth having is worth working for." I said as I gazed into Arlington eyes.

Arlington smiled at me, loosened the grip he had on my hands and reached into the inside pocket of his blazer. I already had everything money could buy. I couldn't imagine what else he could give me. Maybe it was the keys to a Bentley. We talked about it in passing, but did he really go buy me one? I promise if he pulls out the keys to my new car I will scream. The anticipation was killing me.

"Alicia, as I started saying a moment ago, the hell that you sent me through over the past year was worth it. Everything from accusing me of cheating to the situation with AJ, I can finally see things at face value. I love you enough to walk away as a man, loving you and not hating the very thought of you. Here are the divorce papers."

Arlington pulled folded papers from the inside of his blazer, laid them down and slid them across the table to me.

This was not what I was expecting. Arlington and I often joked around, but this was not a joking matter or funny at all. I can't believe that he brought me here to embarrass me like this. I invested too much into him for him to chalk it all up just because he feels sorry for poor little Ms. Piper. With my lips tight I said with anger,

"Oh hell naw Arlington! You will not sit across this table from me and decide what WE are gonna do without my input. I know I might have made a mistake years ago and let my emotions get the best of me, but we are a family now and you aren't gonna walk out on us to be with your hoe."

"You still don't get it. This has nothing to do with Piper, the kids, my boys or your hatin ass friends. This is about me and you, specifically about you being dishonest, about you looking for everyone to take the blame for the things you say and do. Alicia you are a self-centered, vindictive, hopeless-I'm gon' shut up right about now before I really tell you what I think about you."

I looked down at the divorce papers then back up at Arlington. I leaned forward with a stern look on my face I said,

"Piper might have obtained you, but she has no idea how to sustain or maintain what I built. She is too weak of a woman to stand up and push you. You weren't nothing when I met you and you won't be nothing without me. I made you. You had no ambition, no direction, just a functioning alcoholic waiting around for the next party until I gave you a reason to become a positive contributor to society."

Arlington smiled at me as he shook his head.

"I'm glad you said that. And, I hope you got out everything that you needed to say. I refuse to live in misery any longer. I refuse to let you attempt to emasculate me so that you can feel good about you. The truth is, you are unhappy with you and the decisions that you made in your life. You hate Piper because she is the woman that you wish you were.

You know, I never thought about Piper as my woman, but since the very thought of her pisses you off, I think I might just holla at her. You can spend the rest of your life knowing that you sent me into the arms of another woman, a woman that you feel can't hold a candle to you."

I could not believe that he was really trying to elevate this raggedy, weak, gold-digging heffa above me. I don't care what he got to say, he is not going to leave me to take care of these kids by myself so he can go play house. She inherited what she got from her first husband, she is not about to inherit my husband, I ain't dead, buried, or gone.

"Arlington, I think you better rethink your strategy, you ain't running nothing but your mouth. I've molded you into a perfect man. I'll be damned if another woman capitalizes on my investment of hard work, time, sweat, and tears."

Arlington folded his arms and sat back in his chair.

"You are making this easier and easier, keep talking you have my full undivided attention."

I know Arlington was just trying to hurt me but I know he loves me and would never leave me, especially for a bootie call. I'm not gonna play this game with him. These papers he slid me probably aren't even real. This is a test, this is only a test. I reminded myself.

"I'm sorry about all the mean things I just said. Arlington, you are a great man, a loving husband and a dynamic father. I had a bad day and I had no right to take it out on you by saying so many vicious things."

"I'm glad you're sorry but this time, it's not enough."

Arlington stroked his goatee and then folded his hands under his chin as his elbows rested on the table. His stare was piercing and serious.

"After being at the wedding and knowing that I will never be as happy with you as I was the day, we got married helped me decide on the divorce. This is how this is gonna play out. I am divorcing you. We will tell everyone that it just didn't work out. You know, basically that it was a mutual decision to end the relationship. We will never, yes I said we will never tell the truth about why we got a divorce. We're splitting everything down the middle including the children."

I was in total awe as he kept talking.

"Ariah will live with you and AJ is coming to live with me. I thought about this long and hard. AJ is my son, not some strange nigga, and a doctor can't tell me otherwise. I love you enough to never let my son know that his mother is a hoe and has no idea who his biological father is. And, more importantly I love my son enough to be the man and father that I promised him that I would be. I refuse to let my son grow up confused about his identity or become a casualty of decisions. My son will not become a statistic. I owe him that at the very least. Just like you planned to take the lie about AJ's biological father to your grave, we will do just that. If you want me to take both of the kids, I will do that too. But be clear, you do not have any say so about anything else, I am definitely leaving. There is a certain level of shit that I got to deal with from 9 to 5, but I refuse to deal with it at home. I will not pay to be miserable."

I opened the folded stack of papers that were in front of me and glanced over them. The papers were indeed a divorce decree. I was shocked. Tears began to swell in my eyes. Arlington never even noticed. He kept talking.

"I'm not going to spend the next 13 years of my life being unhappy for the sake of the kids. They do what they see us do. Ariah is a princess and should be treated like one. If she sees me treat you like I don't care, then she will allow men to treat her that way. Then I would have to break a fool's neck behind my little girl. AJ will not mistreat a woman because I taught him how to respect a woman. I made sure I considered the best outcome for us all. Last night I burned the test results."

"Arlington are you serious? I know that we can work this out. Despite our problems, we make a good team, we are good together, and we are a family. You are AJ's father the only one he's ever had and the only one he'll ever know."

"No we're not. Let you tell it, everything that we have and everything that we are is because of you. As you put it you are a strong, independent, black woman so be that. I just gotta ask does it feel good to be independent and alone? Since you are so strong, be strong enough to tell me who got you pregnant since I didn't?"

"Does it matter? Why is that something that you need to know?"

"Just as I thought, you have no clue. Well, Alicia this is it. Sign on the dotted line and there will be no need for us to go through an ugly court battle."

I sat starring at the divorce papers while the waiter came to the table to ask if we needed anything else for the evening. I didn't realize how long I was in a trance, just shocked that my perfect life was coming to an end by simply scribing my first and last name on the dotted line of some folded papers. The waiter returned with Arlington's credit card and receipt. After Arlington signed the credit card receipt, he handed me the pen and said,

"Here you go, after you sign this you will no longer have to worry about being married to a sad excuse of a man and you will be alone and independent just like your noisy ass friends. But I guess not, Cassie got a husband and all you have is you."

Without hesitation and in complete silence, I took the pen out of Arlington's hand and signed the divorce decree. At the same time a single tear rolled down my face onto the paper. I folded the papers back up and handed them to Arlington before I patted my face dry with the linen napkin.

Arlington placed the folded papers back into the inside pocket of his blazer.

"Alicia, I will walk you to your truck."

I stood up to leave the restaurant; I was still in shock about what happened this evening. I could not believe that my marriage was really over. As Arlington walked out of the Jharri's towards the door, I held my composure saluting the staff with a smile. Once we got to my truck, Arlington opened the door for me.

"I hope you find what you need in your next relationship. You go ahead home. I've already bought a new house. I will be sending movers over this weekend to retrieve the rest of my things and whatever AJ wants to bring with him. I have already bought him all the things I know he needs for our house. We can work out a schedule for Ariah later, she got a room at my house too. Take care of yourself."

Arlington kissed me on the forehead before he disappeared into the night. I drove home in a complete daze. I pulled into the garage of what was once a happy home and began to try and make sense of what just happened. I walked into the house and noticed that Champaign chilling, music playing, and rose petals everywhere. I completely forgot that I had my assistant set up what I thought was going to be the perfect romantic rendezvous. I made my way to the couch and fell asleep rocking and crying.

The next morning, I was still on the couch completely dressed in what I wore the night before, shoes and all. I thought I was going to spend the day laid up, making up with my husband so I made arrangements not to be in the office that day, I'm glad I did. I was in no shape to face the world. I cried again and again. I couldn't stop myself from crying. It wasn't until noon that I was able to peel myself off the sofa to wash my face.

I decided that I was only going to tell the story once, so I had Myra and Cassie meet me at Ms. Shirley's house. I sent Arlington a text and asked him to get the kids from school; he replied immediately and said that he would just keep them all night. Arlington thought it was best that he stayed with Pops until it was time for him to move out completely. Thank God Arlington wasn't trying to be an ass about the situation. I got to Ms. Shirley's house. The girls were already there.

Everyone was excited and giddy. Cassie had her wedding pictures back and the pictures from her honeymoon. I was not in the mood for this right now.

"Love and marriage doesn't last a lifetime, so cherish those photos. Most likely you will never be that happy while married again." I said as I walked into the kitchen.

"Shut your hatin' ass up. You aren't the only one of us that can have a house, husband and happiness."

"I wish that was the case. Dinner with Arlington was not what I thought it was going to be, we decided that we are getting a divorce. I'm keeping the house, Ariah is going to live with me and AJ will be with him fulltime."

"Oh, my God! Did you agree to this or were you told that you had to agree?" Myra asked as she wrapped her arms around me.

"Put it this way, we did what was best for all concerned parties."

"Well, the bible says they that wait upon the Lord shall renew their strength. When you step out before God look at what happens. Some people believe that God does not approve of divorce. I am here to tell you, when you marry somebody that God didn't send you, you are walking outside of His will anyway and you will be cursed. Ain't that right Ms. Shirley?"

Ms. Shirley looked over her glasses at Myra and just shook her head.

"Honey, you know just enough information to make you stupid. All y'all come sit down at this table and let me teach ya'll silly ass girls a little something."

I don't care how grown you thought you were, in Ms. Shirley's house you had no rights or grown up privileges. We all sat at the table as Cassie closed her photo album in order to give Ms. Shirley her undivided attention.

"I don't know who in the hell taught you girls about love and relationships because ya'll don't have a clue what it is or what you are supposed to do with it. Let me start with you Cassie. Independence is not synonymous with strength, or the symbol of womanhood. In order to be independent, you have to be complete. Just because you're not in a relationship that does not mean you're independent, all that means is you're alone. In a relationship both the man and the woman brings something different to the relationship, something that is needed and desired. Cassie, when you were hurt by your first love and vowed to never hurt like that again, you simultaneously vowed to never love like that again. You disguised your bitterness and hurt with so called independence. It wasn't until you let go of that hurt that you were able to love again. You never know the depth that you can love until you find out how deep you can be hurt. Everything about you reflected your hurt."

We sat in awe as Ms. Shirley continued.

"Cassie, I thank God that you had sense enough to acknowledge and accept a good man. Child let me tell you God prepares the woman for her husband. It wasn't until God saw that you were a complete work of art that He allowed a man to find you. Now thank God for the blessing that He has sent you."

Myra, Cassie and I looked at Ms. Shirley in astonishment. I couldn't believe that she thought Cassie was bitter or needed work. Cassie was single because she had chosen to be. I don't think there is nothing wrong with establishing yourself and having high standards when you decide to choose a man. We let Ms. Shirley continue.

"Cassie, when you gave Alicia advice you gave her advice of hurt, because whatever you are full of is reflected in your words. You made Arlington and every other man that you met responsible for the hurt that Edmond caused you.

You were bound to a hurt that was living happily without you. Not to say he didn't love you, I promise that he has moved on though. You expect all men to be dogs, all men to be dishonest, and all men to cause women to hurt. Alicia might still have her husband if you didn't have your nose in her business. A friend, a true friend will tell you what you need to know not what you want to hear. Ladies there is a distinct difference between a support system and an amen corner."

Cassie looked at me and back at Ms. Shirley,

"Ms. Shirley, if I would have known that I was hurting myself by remembering the hurt, I don't think that it would have taken me so long to get over Edmond."

"I know you didn't share everything about that relationship with me, but it sounds like that man really did love you. He loved you enough to let you go. Cassie you are a smart girl, I don't think it was an accident that you found out that he was married. I believe he thought you would walk away when you figured it out. But when you didn't, he had to hurt you to make you let go. Now that you have been healed, live, love and enjoy your husband every day. Celebrate him as a man, honor him as your husband and you will see that man will go through hell and high water for you."

"Thank you Ms. Shirley, I never thought about it that way. I can say that I feel free. I will remember your advice by not making my husband pay for the hurts of my past."

Cassie said as she nodded at Ms. Shirley. I anxiously sat to see who Ms. Shirley was gonna get next. She repositioned herself in her chair and said,

"Myra, honey Myra. God ain't Santa Clause. He doesn't accept wish lists. Somebody told you what you wanted to hear, and you ran with it without seeking God. Let me tell you something, God is not going to take away somebody's husband to make him yours. You are fearfully and wonderfully made in the image of God. That means you are somebody's rib, not Braxton's. Like I already said, God prepares the woman for the man, not the man for the woman. If you truly believe that God will do exceedingly and abundantly more than what we can ask or think, then why do you think you haven't gotten what you have been waiting for?"

"Ok, Ms. Shirley, for the sake of conversation, Braxton may not be my husband, but I am a godly woman and therefore I am required to be with a godly man. I know I've been called to be a pastor's wife and work beside my husband in ministry. My bible tells me that how can two walk together except they are equally yoked? Therefore, I have the faith that there is some great man of God looking for me. God didn't intend for me to be with a man that is not saved. I can't receive what you are saying. This man that was trying to date me is an architect and does a drive by to see God a couple times a year and I am supposed to accept that? No, I rebuke that in the name of Jesus. I refuse to settle."

"Myra you are at church every time the doors open and yet you don't know that Lord as your personal savior. The word says let this mind be in you which is also in Christ Jesus. You can't show me where Jesus turned sinners away. I promise I can show you where Jesus welcomed them, where He dwelled with them. Listen to me little girl, Elder Mack was not always saved. I'm pretty sure your momma will tell you that your daddy wasn't always saved either. Elder Mack was a construction worker that stopped by the bar every day for a beer with the men from work. The first time I met him, I knew he had a call on his life. The church was not where he wanted to be and the thought of Jesus never entered his mind. I decided to minister to him by letting him see the goodness of Jesus in me, by letting him feel the love of Jesus on him. As time went on his curiosity about the Lord turned into a lifestyle. Once he got saved then we got married, a yoke is nothing more than a mindset. Until we got the same mindset we could not be joined together."

As Ms. Shirley talked, Myra kept looking away pretending that Ms. Shirley's words were not piercing. I now know what the scripture means when it says; the word will cut like a two edge sword. I know Myra is being cut deep right about now. I just knew Myra was about to say something because she will debate the bible like she wrote it herself. But much to my surprise she listened and didn't say a word.

"Honey I'm only telling you this for your own good. If all you do is surround yourself with church folk, how are you winning souls for the Lord? When was the last time you saw fruit in your life. Misery, loneliness, and confusion ain't fruit. There is power in the name of Jesus. It's time for you to take dominion over something other than a committee meeting and learn more about the Lord than them cliché scriptures. Or, you will die an old bitter woman destined for hell. Despite you serving the Lord, loving the Lord is what will get you in heaven. He said if you love me, you will keep my commandments and baby let me tell you obedience is a commandment. There is a difference between good and God. You ain't no different from Cassie. She used independence as an excuse not to love and you are using God. Love yourself enough to receive God's love from a man. You are worthy to be loved. Braxton ain't your husband and neither is the Lord."

Now Myra was fighting her tears shaking her head in agreement with Ms. Shirley. Maybe that girl will finally find happiness for the first time in her life. I don't think she has ever felt the comfort of a man's arms. I pray that she listens and applies what Ms. Shirley said.

"I tried to tell ya'll Ms. Shirley don't pull no punches. You better take what she says at face value."

Ms. Shirley's countenance changed. She just glared at me like I had said or done something wrong. Sitting in the chair she put her hand on her hip and extended her right hand with her index finger pointing straight at me.

"Missy I'm real good and tired of you right about now. I have been trying to hold my peace, but it is time somebody told you the truth about you. You are just rotten to the core. You think that you are the reason that the sun rises and sets every day. You are so damn evil that you destroy everything good that comes your way. You never wanted Arlington, kids, or this life you created, you just wanted to think you had something that nobody else had. You feel like you are superior to everybody else when the fact is you add no value to people's lives. You don't know the value of a good man. You had no idea what to do with Arlington, that's why you misused him."

I was taken back by Ms. Shirley, she was mad at me, for what I had no clue. Maybe she was just on a roll. I guess the last one gets it the worse.

"Ms. Shirley, why are you mad at me? I listen to you. You out of all people know that Arlington would be in the gutter right now if it wasn't for me. When he got me, he had a wife that can handle her own, while giving him a hand up."

"You are just a lying wonder! You don't think you can do no wrong, you think everything is everybody else's fault. You lied to get Arlington, you lied to keep him, and you are lying about why you are losing him. Baby, what doesn't come out in the wash, will come out in the rinse. If you ain't honest with nobody else, be honest with yourself. God knows your heart. Why did you pick Arlington out the gutter as you put it, only to keep reminding him about where he came from? And, every opportunity you get, you try to knock him back down there. You want to be married, but you have no idea or desire to be a wife."

I refused to take this hit for the team. I need to let Ms. Shirley know that I was following Cassie and Myra's advice.

"I only followed the advice that was given to me. I guess bad advice shouldn't have a voice. My marriage was and still is important to me that was why I asked people for help because I don't have all the answers."

"This is the shit I'm talking about. Please forgive me Lord. Girl you don' made me cuss. You seem to find the short comings in everybody. What do you ever do wrong? You are a liar and the truth ain't in you. What's sad is you don't even realize that you are even lying. You can't expect people to give you sound advice when you don't tell the truth.

Folks can only go by the information that you gave them. You ask for advice so that folks will agree with you, to make you feel good about the decision that you chose to make. Listen to me and listen to me good. You will harvest every one of the seeds that you have sown. There is a reckoning day for everybody. I just pray that the Lord has mercy on your soul."

"Ms. Shirley what have I done that is so terribly wrong? I have accomplished every goal that I have set for myself. How many people can say that?"

"What does it profit a man to gain the world and lose his soul? You lost a good man and a happy home because you refuse to listen, support, or contribute. Tell me Alicia how it feels to have your life slide through your fingers like grains of salt?"

I was waiting for my girls to jump in and help a sista out but they sat there, like they were scared they were gonna get a whoopin or something. I had nothing to say because Ms. Shirley is old but she don't know everything. But I for damn sure ain't about to sit around and get beat up for nothing. I grabbed my keys that were lying on the table.

"Baby you can run but you can't hide from the truth."

Myra and Cassie took this as their out as well. I noticed them giving each other the "you get up first" eyes.

Before I headed to the door, Ms. Shirley said,

"Ya'll don' worried me to death, I got to take one of my pressure pills and go lay down. Let yourselves out. I swear before God, ya'll are a different breed of women. Cassie seems like she is the only one that had sense enough to get herself together before it was too late. I'm going to watch my show. Bye."

Ms. Shirley really did just get up, shaking her head and left us in the kitchen. Once she got out of ear shot Cassie said,

"I'm leaving while I'm in her good graces. I ain't trying to get caught up with you and Myra. I'm glad DJ had the patience to love me pass my hurt. I will learn from the mistakes that I see other people make in their marriages to improve mine."

"Just because you been married for 10 minutes doesn't mean that you are an expert. Don't go judge me because of what Ms. Shirley had to say."

"Don't be mad at me because you hate your life. What I've to this point didn't work, so I have nothing to lose by following Ms. Shirley's advice. Besides she was successfully married until her husband passed away apparently, she knows what she's talking about."

I couldn't believe that Cassie was really acting like she knew what she was talking about. I'm just gonna sit back and let her see for herself. I will make sure that I remind her about what she said.

Myra still didn't have much to say as we all exited Ms. Shirley's house. People have always used kit gloves when dealing with Myra because she starts arguing with scripture and people generally just back away from her. I'm glad that Ms. Shirley got on her. Myra is a good woman and does deserve happiness. I hope she takes Ms. Shirley's advice to heart and realizes that neither Jesus nor Braxton is her husband.

"Myra girl, are you gonna be ok."

"Yes, ma'am I'm good."

"I just need to go home and meditate on the things that Ms. Shirley had to say. I will be fine."

The girls and I hugged good bye and left Ms. Shirley's house. There was nothing for me to do but go home. There was no kids, no Arlington just me and a bottle of wine. I was going to relax and unwind. I did just that. There is nothing like a hot bath, full of thick, fluffy bubbles to bring serenity. At that moment, the fact that I was getting a divorce didn't matter. I was not trying to keep somebody that wasn't trying to be kept.

It would only be a matter of time before Arlington remembered the luxuries that came with having a wife. No more warm body at night, no more additional income, and no one to clean up behind him. I don't believe that he will even send the papers to the court.

The weekend was here. Time for Arlington to get his crap out my house, I wish he would take everything that way I can get me some new furniture. Just to make sure that there was no drama, I left home before Arlington and the movers showed up. I took the kids to the museum. I wanted to spend as much time as I could with them so the transition of the divorce would be seamless. I was grateful that Arlington bought a house in the subdivision across the street from where we were already living.

That meant AJ would not have to change schools and once the kids got a lot older they could bike or walk between the two houses. Arlington and I hadn't decided when and what we were telling the kids about the divorce, but it was something that we needed to handle fairly soon. I think I will suggest to him that we would tell the kids about our new living situation after church on Sunday.

Spending an entire day out with the kids was much more than what I bargained for. They wore me out. The running, bickering, and asking questions were working my nerves. I couldn't help but chuckle to myself. I think Arlington bit off more than he could chew by wanting to be a fulltime, single father. I think when he has to be responsible for everything from getting AJ ready for school in the morning, to attending games, dealing with a sick child and still maintaining a job will make him rethink his strategy and put all this nonsense behind us.

I received a text from Arlington when they were done moving, the kids and I were beat. AJ and Ariah were so tired that they didn't notice that their father wasn't home. I was not going to fight with them. I let them go to sleep without taking their baths. After getting the kids in bed, I walked through the house to see what Arlington left behind.

Much to my surprise everything from his clothes out his drawers to his tools in the garage was gone. I walked into the kitchen for a cup of tea before lying down. On the island in the kitchen was Arlington's keys and garage door opener. What a dramatic touch. The only reason he left this stuff is for an excuse for me not having access to his house.

No telling what hoes he was going to have over there but I was happy he gave me the keys, now I don't have to worry about him thinking he was running stuff over here.

Sunday morning Arlington came to pick me and the kids up for church. This was going to be our last time attending church together as a family, at least for a while. The church service was great, I guess. My focus was on having the conversation with the kids after church. We went to have a late lunch after service. The restaurant was where Arlington thought it would be good to tell the kids that we weren't going to live together anymore. He said we needed to do this in a neutral place so that the kids won't associate home with the bad memory. I have no idea where he got concept from but whatever.

Arlington signaled to me that he was about to tell the kids what was going on. Since this was his decision, I thought he should be the one to tell them. If they got angry at anybody at least they would be angry at him.

"Guess what kids, Mommy and daddy have decided that we are going to live in two houses."

Before Arlington could finish, AJ sucked his teeth, rolled his eyes, and said,

"Again dad, for how long this time? I don't want to keep moving my stuff."

Arlington cleared his throat before responding,

"You don't have to move anything. I have taken care of everything; you guys will keep the rooms at home that you already have. But, you will also have a room at daddy's house too. But AJ you are going to sleep at my house and visit mom, Ariah you get to stay with mommy and visit me and AJ"

AJ was excited, but Ariah was sad.

"What's wrong punkin? Why do you have a sad face?" I asked Ariah.

"It's not fair, why does AJ get to go with daddy and I have to stay with you?"

Arlington looked at me, then answered her for me.

"I wanted both of you to live at my house but somebody has to stay and take care of mommy but the good news is you now have two of everything. You have two houses, two rooms, and guess what two bikes."

Ariah was excited but, she started back coloring, like we hadn't said anything. At ages 7 and 8, I think I have the smartest kids in the world. The kids were so excited about seeing their second house that they went home with Arlington. I'm glad he took them so I can get some things arranged in the house so I could start my work week on a good note.

When I made it home, the house was empty and cold. The mere shadows were only reminders of happiness and joy that accented my home. I guess this is it, I thought to myself. I took care of things in the house and went to bed happy.

A couple months had passed, the kids were well adjusted to the new living situation and new schedule. I was so busy at work and my other community obligations that I hadn't thought too much about Arlington. Other than a few quick lunches; I hadn't spent time with Myra and Cassie either. I saw Ms. Shirley a couple times a week. She still babysat for me, but I made sure that I was in and out of there before she could share any of her so called wisdom with me.

I only saw Arlington in passing. He was trying to be superdad. He was coaching AJ's basketball team and volunteering in Ariah's classroom twice a month. The kids hadn't mentioned a female yet. That only meant one thing, he was building his case so I would let him come back home. I was proud of him for taking such an active role in the kid's lives, but he couldn't keep up this charade forever. I know he loves me and it was eating him up that I hadn't asked him to come home.

It was Friday night and I was ready to go blow off some steam. I called Cassie so she could meet me for happy hour.

"Hey Lady, it's Friday also known as Martini Day. Let's go have a few drinks and talk about these sorry men."

"You know you are my girl, but I have to pass this time. I got wife stuff this evening. DJ has a work thing going on and the part of his beautiful, dutiful wife will be played by me. Besides that, we got a full day tomorrow, doing some home improvement stuff at the house."

"For real Cassie, you haven't been married a year yet and you have already let that fool change you. I thought you were your own woman."

"When I got married I was supposed to change. I'm still my own woman but, I'm a wife first. I enjoy spending time with my husband. I'm excited that I get to spend time with my husband."

"You better be careful the next thing you know, he will be asking you to give up your career to bare his youngins."

"And what's wrong with that. If he decides that he doesn't want me to work and that we are ready to start a family, then so be it. I know he knows what he is doing and I will be provided for."

Oh my God, I could not believe that I as actually hearing this come out of Cassie mouth. Now that she got a husband she was trying to act brand new.

"You aren't being a good friend. I never put Arlington before you. And if I recall, I had drinks with you when DJ was dogging you out when ya'll were dating back in the day."

"Don't try to play the friend card. Don't be mad at me because you didn't prioritize being a wife and set boundaries with your friends. If you did maybe, you would still be married. Why can't you just be happy for me? I gotta get dressed now. I'll holla back."

"Whatever Cassie bye." I hung up the phone. Cassie was really on one. But she will see in due time. When the "honeymoon" is over and DJ shows his true colors, all I can do is be a friend and try not to say I told you so. I guess I will call Myra and go get a cup of coffee.

"Myra, get off the couch and come have coffee with me." I said.

"I would love to but I'm about to meet Darryl for dinner, maybe tomorrow though."

"Who is Darryl?"

"Remember the architect? He and I bumped into each other at the bank and we have been on a few dates. I completely brushed him off back then. When we saw each other, I was surprised that he was still interested. Praise the Lord for second chances. He's a great guy. I can't wait for you to meet him."

"Ok, have fun. I will check in tomorrow to see how your date went."

"Talk to you then."

What is the world coming too? First Cassie gets married now Myra is doing more than fantasizing about Braxton. Since I didn't have anyone to hang out with, I decided to go home. Since it was still fairly early in the evening, I decided to go through the stack of mail that had piled up on the desk this week. There was a letter from the court. I didn't have any tickets; I was curious to see what was in the envelope.

My heart stopped, as I began to read. It was an official dissolution of marriage. My marriage to Arlington was officially over. Until this moment, it didn't seem real. My marriage was really over. I couldn't believe that it was really over. My marriage was really over. I thought if I kept repeating it to myself, I would believe it. Once I believed it, maybe I could accept it. I sat on the sofa and realized that I was alone. Nobody was there to comfort me, nobody cared that I was hurting, nobody was here for me.

The doorbell rang. I could not imagine who would be at my house. Much to my surprise, it was my mother. As soon as I saw her, I started crying. I let her in and we sat in the family room.

"I saw Arlington's father at the store, and he told me that Arlington moved out and took AJ with him. He assumed I already knew. Why didn't you tell me what was going on?"

"I was ashamed and trying to prove to the world that I was independent."

"Despite what you think, everybody needs somebody. So how long is the separation?"

I handed my mom the envelope.

"The divorce was final yesterday."

"Listen to me little girl, never make a permanent decision from a temporary location because some things you can't take back."

"Arlington left me and there is no chance that it will ever be reconciled."

"I don't know what happened or why, but I can tell you this. When you disguise the truth with what you feel and act on your emotions the problem gets worse because when your emotions change so will your decisions. When you react instead of respond, chances are you will regret your actions. Baby emotions lie. Our emotions are evidence of our past and encompass all of who we are, what we've been through, not just what we are dealing with in the moment. What that means is our emotions act like filters, we see things according to what happened the last time, what isn't resolved, and what we are entitled to feel."

I don't give a damn what my mother is saying right now.

"Mom feelings are valid even though others might not agree with you."

My mom smirked,

"Are your feelings valid? Or is something else the catalyst to make you feel a certain way? When you figure out how to control your emotions, you'll make wiser decisions. Always acknowledge what you feel and respond with wisdom. I challenge you to ask yourself, do you really want Arlington? Or, do you want the prestige that marriage brings?"

I was for real ready for her to go now. I stood up. Hopefully my mom would get the hint and immediately get her some ghost.

"Ok, I can take a hint. No problem daughter I will leave, I've already spoke my piece, you know where to find me, when you are ready to handle this like a smart adult instead of an independent fool."

"Goodbye mother." I said, as I shut the door behind her.

Listening to my mom made me realize that I should not be sitting here wallowing in self-pity. I didn't need anybody to go out and have fun. I am woman enough to be alone. I got dressed and decided to step out on the town. I had the music blaring in the truck. I was singing along getting hyped up. I hadn't partied at a club in years, but no time like the present to get back on that horse.

As I was getting onto the highway, my life flashed before my eyes. I saw Arlington, the kids, and Piper drive pass heading in the opposite direction. At that moment reality set in for me. This was Piper and Arlington's plan along. If that bitch think I'm gonna let her steal my family. She got another thing coming. This ain't a damn movie, Piper will not ride off into the sunset with what's rightfully mine.

......to be continued

About the Author

Deondriea Cantrice is a student of the human condition, wielding the written craft to captivate the mind much like an artist wields a brush. The pages are a blank canvas on which to draw from a talent heralded by many and matched only by an imagination that rises to the task.

Deondriea developed her writing skills in high school and sharpened her literary skills by writing newsletters, short stories, program curriculum, and most notably, When Emotions Lie.

Now Certified Confidence and Transitional Life Coach, Deondriea provides tailored guidance, inspiring clients to shed self-doubt and embrace their true potential. Her sessions are a blend of motivational dialogue and actionable steps, designed to equip individuals with the tools needed for unwavering self-belief. She aspires to entertain, educate, and inspire her readers with tales of true life.

Deondriea greets everyone with a smile and aims to have a positive impact on everyone she encounters through effective communication, affirmative interaction and veracity. Deondriea believes, "with direction and discipline, accomplishment is attainable."

Can two people really be two halves of the same whole? If so Sterling and Sheridyn are a perfect fit. After experiencing one betrayal after another, Sterling puts his heart under lock and key. Is he willing to grant Sheridyn access to the place that no one can enter? When Sterling and Sheridyn's worlds collide, will they be able to control their passion? Or will their seductive dance burn up on flames? *Rhythm Can't Keep Time* is not a sappy love story or an unrealistic male bashing narrative, but an exploration of love through an erotic lens.

PICK UP YOUR COPY, TODAY!

@deondriea

@deondriea

@deondriea

@deondriea

@deondriea

@deondriea